LANGENSCHEIDT-LEKTÜRE 42
SHORT STORIES

Weitere Titel dieser Reihe:

ENGLISCH

4	**Strange Adventures**	Abenteuergeschichten, die sich besonderer Beliebtheit erfreuen.
13	**Dreizehn Whodunits**	Kriminalgeschichten u. a. von Agatha Christie, O. Henry und Saki.
15	**Laugh and be merry**	Köstlicher britischer Humor in Short Stories und Witzen.
42	**Short Stories**	Ausgesuchte Erzählungen, die sich durch ihren hervorragenden Stil auszeichnen.
60	**Humorous Short Stories**	Spaßige Situationskomik und amüsante Schlaglichter auf englische Originalität.
61	**The Birds/Kiss Me Again, Stranger**	Hier — die Vorlage für Hitchcocks Thriller, dazu ein weiterer Shocker.
66	**A Steinbeck Reader**	Vier Kurzgeschichten des großen amerikanischen Erzählers.
67	**Murder! Murder? Murder!**	Fünf Mordgeschichten und fünf ungewöhnliche Täter — besonders spannende Lektüre.

FRANZÖSISCH

44	**Nouvelles françaises**	Eine Sammlung literarisch interessanter französischer Novellen.
57	**Textes Français Modernes**	Humoristische und ernste „Auskünfte" über historische und kulturgeschichtliche Themen.
62	**Thanatos Palace Hotel**	Novellistische Kostbarkeiten, wie sie nur aus der Feder André Maurois' fließen können.
63	**Fête-Dieu**	Vielfarbige Skizzen Marcel Jouhandeaus aus dem französischen Provinzleben vom Mystisch-Traumhaften bis hin zum „esprit gaulois".
68	**Humour à gogo**	Typische Witze sind in diesem Lektüreband mit humorvollen Kurzgeschichten vereinigt.

ITALIENISCH

7	**Un po' di tutto**	Aktuelle Einblicke in die Verhältnisse des Landes und in das Geistesleben des Volkes.
21	**Novelle italiane**	Unterhaltende Beiträge bekannter italienischer Novellisten.
64	**Troppo Ricca**	Alberto Moravia — der sicher bekannteste italienische Schriftsteller —, hier der Autor wirkungsvoll pointierter Erzählungen.
69	**Storie criminali**	Moderne italienische Kriminalgeschichten — sie halten den Leser bis zur letzten Zeile gefangen.

RUSSISCH

55	**Moderne russische Erzählungen**	Typische Kurzgeschichten, teils humoristisch, teils ernst.
56	**Leichte russische Kurzgeschichten**	Populäre Aufsätze, Anekdoten, Sprichwörter und Kurzgeschichten.

SPANISCH

36	**Cuentos Españoles**	Charakteristische Erzählungen aus dem spanischen Volksleben.
58	**Lecturas Amenas**	Humorvolle Erzählungen in spanischer Umgangssprache.
65	**Rodando por España**	Interessante Einblicke in das Alltagsleben des spanischen Volkes.

Langenscheidt-Lektüre 42

Short Stories

Sechs repräsentative englische Kurzgeschichten
von John Galsworthy, Arnold Bennett u.a.

[redacted]

LANGENSCHEIDT
BERLIN · MÜNCHEN · WIEN · ZÜRICH

Inhaltsverzeichnis

[redacted]

Auflage: 8. 7. 6. 5. | *Letzte Zahlen*
Jahr: 1978 77 76 | *maßgeblich*

Druck: Druckhaus Langenscheidt, Berlin-Schöneberg
Printed in Germany · ISBN 3-468-44420-6

Vorwort

Die Beliebtheit der Reihe „Langenscheidts fremdsprachliche Lektüre“ veranlaßte den Verlag, nun auch die „Short Stories“ in einer überarbeiteten Fassung vorzulegen.

Die Auswahl bietet eine Einführung in die für die englische und amerikanische Literatur so charakteristische Gattung der „Short Story“, die sich durch realistische Erzählweise und Handlungsbetontheit auszeichnet.

Die „Short Stories“ wurden kritisch durchgesehen. Neue Illustrationen und eine moderne Gestaltung des Druckbildes geben dem Band ein neues Gesicht.

Die Vokabelspalten wurden gründlich überarbeitet und ergänzt, so daß die Texte jetzt auch Lesern mit geringeren Vorkenntnissen zugänglich sind. Die Aussprache ist in internationaler Lautschrift angegeben.

Auch diese Sammlung soll dem Leser die Möglichkeit bieten, seine Sprachkenntnisse in unterhaltsamer Weise aufzufrischen und zu erweitern.

DER VERLAG

Erklärung der Aussprachebezeichnung

A. Vokale und Diphthonge

[ɑ:] reines langes a, wie in Vater, kam, Schwan: *far* [fɑ:], *father* ['fɑ:ðə].

[ʌ] kommt im Deutschen nicht vor. Kurzes dunkles a, bei dem die Lippen nicht gerundet sind. Vorn und offen gebildet: *butter* ['bʌtə], *come* [kʌm], *colour* ['kʌlə], *blood* [blʌd], *flourish* ['flʌriʃ], *twopence* ['tʌpəns].

[æ] heller, ziemlich offener, nicht zu kurzer Laut. Raum zwischen Zunge und Gaumen noch größer als bei ä in Ähre: *fat* [fæt], *man* [mæn].

[ɛə] nicht zu offenes halblanges ä; im Englischen nur vor r, das als ein dem ä nachhallendes ə erscheint: *bare* [bɛə], *pair* [pɛə], *there* [ðɛə].

[ai] Bestandteile: helles, zwischen ɑ: und æ liegendes a und schwächeres offenes i. Die Zunge hebt sich halbwegs zur i-Stellung: *I* [ai], *lie* [lai], *dry* [drai].

[au] Bestandteile: helles, zwischen ɑ: und æ liegendes a und schwächeres offenes u: *house* [haus], *now* [nau].

[ei] halboffenes e, nach i auslautend, indem die Zunge sich halbwegs zur i-Stellung hebt: *date* [deit], *play* [plei], *obey* [ə'bei].

[e] halboffenes kurzes e, etwas geschlossener als das e in Bett: *bed* [bed], *less* [les].

[ə] flüchtiger Gleitlaut, ähnlich dem deutschen, flüchtig gesprochenen e in Gelage: *about* [ə'baut], *butter* ['bʌtə], *connect* [kə'nekt].

[i:] langes i, wie in lieb, Bibel, aber etwas offener einsetzend als im Deutschen; wird in Südengland doppellautig gesprochen, indem sich die Zunge allmählich zur i-Stellung hebt: *scene* [si:n], *sea* [si:], *feet* [fi:t], *ceiling* ['si:liŋ].

[i] kurzes offenes i wie in bin, mit: *big* [big], *city* ['siti].

[iə] halboffenes halblanges i mit nachhallendem ə: *here* [hiə], *hear* [hiə], *inferior* [in'fiəriə].

[ou] halboffenes langes o, in schwaches u auslautend; keine Rundung der Lippen, kein Heben der Zunge: *note* [nout], *boat* [bout], *below* [bi'lou].

[ɔ:] offener langer, zwischen a und o schwebender Laut: *fall* [fɔ:l], *nought* [nɔ:t], *or* [ɔ:], *before* [bi'fɔ:].

[ɔ] offener kurzer, zwischen a und o schwebender Laut, offener als das o in Motte: *god* [gɔd], *not* [nɔt], *wash* [wɔʃ], *hobby* ['hɔbi].

[ɔi] Bestandteile: offenes o und schwächeres offenes i. Die Zunge hebt sich halbwegs zur i-Stellung: *voice* [vɔis], *boy* [bɔi], *annoy* [ə'nɔi].

[əː] im Deutschen fehlender Laut; offenes langes ö, etwa wie gedehnt gesprochenes ö in öffnen, Mörder; kein Vorstülpen oder Runden der Lippen, kein Heben der Zunge: *word* [wəːd], *girl* [gəːl], *learn* [ləːn], *murmur* ['məːmə].

[uː] langes u wie in Buch, doch ohne Lippenrundung; vielfach diphthongisch als halboffenes langes u mit nachhallendem geschlossenen u: *fool* [fuːl], *shoe* [ʃuː], *you* [juː], *rule* [ruːl] *canoe* [kə'nuː].

[uə] halboffenes halblanges u mit nachhallendem ə: *poor* [puə], *sure* [ʃuə], *allure* [ə'ljuə].

[u] flüchtiges u: *put* [put], *look* [luk], *careful* ['kɛəful].

Die **Länge eines Vokals** wird durch [:] bezeichnet, z. B. *ask* [ɑːsk], *astir* [ə'stəː]. Die **Betonung** der englischen Wörter wird durch das Zeichen ['] vor der zu betonenden Silbe angegeben, z. B. *onion* ['ʌnjən].

B. Konsonanten

[r] nur vor Vokalen gesprochen. Völlig verschieden vom deutschen Zungenspitzen- oder Zäpfchen-r. Die Zungenspitze bildet mit der oberen Zahnwulst eine Enge, durch die der Ausatmungsstrom mit Stimmton hindurchgetrieben wird, ohne den Laut zu rollen. Am Ende eines Wortes wird r nur bei Bindung mit dem Anlautvokal des folgenden Wortes gesprochen: *rose* [rouz], *pride* [praid], *there is* [ðɛər'iz].

[ʒ] stimmhaftes sch, wie g in Genie, j in Journal: *azure* ['æʒə], *jazz* [dʒæz], *jeep* [dʒiːp], *large* [lɑːdʒ].

[ʃ] stimmloses sch, wie im Deutschen Schnee, rasch: *shake* [ʃeik], *washing* ['wɔʃiŋ], *lash* [læʃ].

[θ] im Deutschen nicht vorhandener stimmloser Lispellaut; durch Anlegen der Zunge an die oberen Schneidezähne hervorgebracht: *thin* [θin], *path* [pɑːθ], *method* ['meθəd].

[ð] derselbe Laut stimmhaft, d.h. mit Stimmton: *there* [ðɛə], *breathe* [briːð], *father* ['fɑːðə].

[s] stimmloser Zischlaut, entsprechend dem deutschen ß in Spaß, reißen: *see* [siː], *hats* [hæts], *decide* [di'said].

[z] stimmhafter Zischlaut wie im Deutschen sausen: *zeal* [ziːl], *rise* [raiz], *horizon* [hə'raizn].

[ŋ] wird wie der deutsche Nasenlaut in fangen, singen gebildet: *ring* [riŋ], *singer* ['siŋə].

[ŋk] derselbe Laut mit nachfolgendem k wie im Deutschen senken, Wink: *ink* [iŋk], *tinker* ['tiŋkə].

[w] flüchtiges, mit Lippe an Lippe gesprochenes w, aus der Mundstellung für u: gebildet: *will* [wil], *swear* [swɛə], *queen* [kwiːn].

[f] stimmloser Lippenlaut wie im Deutschen flott: *fat* [fæt], *tough* [tʌf], *effort* ['efət].

[v] stimmhafter Lippenlaut wie im Deutschen Vase, Ventil: *vein* [vein], velvet ['velvit].

[j] flüchtiger, zwischen j und i schwebender Laut: *onion* ['ʌnjən], *yes* [jes], *filial* ['filjəl].

Abkürzungen

AE amerikanisches Englisch
BE britisches Englisch
e-e eine
e-m einem
e-n einen
e-s eines
etw. etwas
F familiär, Umgangssprache
Frz. französisch
j-d jemand
j-m jemandem
j-n jemanden
j-s jemandes
o.s. *oneself*
Pl. Plural, Mehrzahl
s.b. *somebody*
sl. *slang*
Span. spanisch
s.th. *something*
V vulgär

The Choice

By J. Galsworthy

Some years ago in Chelsea there used to stand at the crossing of a street leading to the Embankment an old man whose living was derived from the cleanliness of boots. In the intervals of plying his broom he could generally be seen seated on an upturned wooden box, talking to an Irish terrier, who belonged to a house nearby, and had taken a fancy to him. He was a Cornishman by birth, had been a plumber by trade, and was a cheerful, independent old fellow with ruddy cheeks, grey hair and beard, and little, bright, rather watery, grey eyes. But he was a great sufferer from a variety of ailments. He had gout, and some trouble in his side, and feet that were like barometers in their susceptibility to weather.

Of all these matters he would speak to us in a very impersonal and uncomplaining way, diagnosing himself, as it were, for the benefit of his listeners. He was, it seems, alone in the world, not having of course at that time anything to look forward to in the way of a pension, nor, one fancies, very much to look back on except the death of his near relatives and the decline of the plumbing trade. It had declined him for years, but, even before a long illness ousted him in favour of younger men, he had

choice [tʃɔis] *Wahl*
Chelsea ['tʃelsi] *Stadtteil in London*
(he) used to (do) [ju:st] *(er) pflegte zu (tun)*
crossing ['krɔsiŋ] *(Straßen)Kreuzung*
Embankment [im'bæŋkmənt] *Uferstraße*
living ['liviŋ] *Unterhalt*
be derived [di'raivd] *herstammen*
cleanliness ['klenlinis] *Sauberkeit*
interval ['intəvəl] *Pause*
ply [plai] *handhaben*
broom [brum] *Besen*
upturn [ʌp'tə:n] *umkippen, hochstellen*
belong [bi'lɔŋ] *gehören*
take a fancy to ['fænsi] *Zuneigung fassen zu*
Cornishman ['kɔ:niʃmən] *Mann aus Cornwall*
by birth [bə:θ] *von Geburt*
plumber ['plʌmə] *Klempner*
by trade [treid] *von Beruf*
ruddy ['rʌdi] *rötlich, gesund*
be a sufferer from ['sʌfərə] *leiden an*
variety [və'raiəti] *Reihe*
ailment ['eilmənt] *Leiden*
gout [gaut] *Gicht*
trouble ['trʌbl] *Leiden*
susceptibility [səseptə'biliti] *Empfindlichkeit*
uncomplaining ['ʌnkəm'pleiniŋ] *ohne Murren*
diagnose ['daiəgnouz] *(Krankheit) bestimmen*
as it were *gleichsam*
for the benefit of ['benifit] *zum Besten von*
look forward to ['fɔ:wəd] *sich freuen auf*
fancy ['fænsi] *sich vorstellen*
relative ['relətiv] *Verwandte(r)*

felt very severely the palpable difference in things.

This long illness and the death of his wife coming close together (and sweeping away the last of his savings), had determined him therefore to buy a broom and seek for other occupation. To sweep a crossing was not a profession that he himself would have chosen before all others, still it was "better than the house—and you were your own master". The climate in those days not being the most suitable for a business which necessitated constant exposure to all elements but that of fire, his ailments were proportionally active; but the one remarkable feature of his perpetual illness was that he was always "better" than he had been. We could not at times help thinking that this continual crescendo of good health should have gradually raised him to a pinnacle of paramount robustness; and it was with a certain disappointment, in the face of his assurances, that we watched him getting, on the contrary, slowly stiffer and feebler, and noted the sure increase of the egg-like deposits, which he would proudly have us remark, about his wrists and fingers.

He was so entirely fixed and certain that he was "going in the river" before he went "in the house", that one hesitated to suggest that the time was at hand when he should cease to expose himself all day and every day. He had evidently pondered long and with a certain deep philos-

decline [di'klain] *Niedergang; bedrücken*
oust [aust] *verdrängen*
in favour of ['feivə] *zugunsten (von)*

---

severe [si'viə] *hart*
palpable ['pælpəbl] *fühl-, greifbar*
savings *Pl.* ['seiviŋz] *Ersparnisse*
determine [di'tə:min] *j-n veranlassen*
profession [prə'feʃən] *Beruf*
chosen ['tʃouzn] *gewählt*
house *hier: Armenhaus*
climate ['klaimit] *Umstände*
suitable ['sju:təbl] *geeignet*
necessitate [ni'sesiteit] *erfordern*
exposure [iks'pouʒə] *Ausgesetztsein*
proportionally [prə'pɔ:ʃnəli] *im Verhältnis*
feature ['fi:tʃə] *Merkmal*
perpetual [pə'petjuəl] *andauernd*
continual [kən'tinjuəl] *fortwährend*
crescendo [kri'ʃendou] *Anwachsen, Zunahme*
gradual ['grædjuəl] *allmählich*
pinnacle ['pinəkl] *Höhepunkt*
paramount ['pærəmaunt] *höchst*
disappointment [disə'pɔintmənt] *Enttäuschung*
in the face of [feis] *angesichts*
assurance [ə'ʃuərəns] *Ver-, Zusicherung*
on the contrary ['kɔntrəri] *im Gegenteil*
feeble ['fi:bl] *schwach*
increase ['inkri:s] *Wachsen, Vergrößerung*
deposit [di'pɔzit] *Ablagerung*
wrist [rist] *Handgelenk*
fix [fiks] *richten auf*
hesitate ['heziteit] *zögern*
suggest [sə'dʒest] *andeuten*
at hand *nahe*
cease [si:z] *aufhören*

ophy on this particular subject, and fortified himself by hearsay.

"The house ain't for a man that respects himself", he would remark. And, since that was his conviction, such as respected themselves could not very well beg him to act against it. At the same time, it became increasingly difficult to pass him without wondering how much longer it would be before he finally sought shelter in the element of water, which was so apt to pour down on him day by day.

It is uncertain whether he discussed this matter of the river versus the house with the dog, to whom he was always talking; but that they shared a certain fellow-feeling on the subject of exposure and advancing age is more than probable; for as he would point out: The poor old feller's teeth were going; and the stiffness across his loins was always worse when it was wet. In fact, he was afraid that the old dog was getting old! And the dog would sit patiently for an hour at a time looking up at him, trying to find out, perhaps, from his friend's face what a dog should do, when the enemy weighed on him till he could no longer tolerate himself, not knowing, of course, that kindly humans would see to it that he did not suffer more than a dog could bear. On his face with its grizzled muzzle and rheumy eyes, thus turned up, there was never a sign of debate, it was full of confidence that, whatever decision his friend came to, in this momentous

expose o. s. [iks'pouz] *sich aussetzen*
ponder ['pɔndə] *nachdenken*
philosophy [fi'lɔsəfi] *Philosophie*

---

particular [pə'tikjulə] *besonder*
subject ['sʌbdʒikt] *Thema*
fortify ['fɔːtifai] *stärken, ermutigen*
hearsay ['hiəsei] *Hörensagen*
ain't V [eint] = is not
since [sins] *da, weil*
conviction [kən'vikʃən] *Überzeugung*
such as *diejenigen, die*
increasing [in'kriːsiŋ] *zunehmend*
wonder ['wʌndə] *sich fragen*
sought [sɔːt] *suchte*
shelter ['ʃeltə] *Schutz*
apt [æpt] *geeignet, geneigt*
pour down [pɔː] *sich ergießen*
versus ['vəːsəs] *gegen*
share [ʃɛə] *teilen*
fellow-feeling ['felou-'fiːliŋ] *Gefühl der Verbundenheit*
advance [əd'vaːns] *fortschreiten*
probable ['prɔbəbl] *wahrscheinlich*
feller F = fellow
loins *Pl.* [lɔinz] *Lenden*
worse [wəːs] *schlimmer*
wet [wet] *naß*
patient ['peiʃənt] *geduldig*
weigh [wei] *lasten*
tolerate ['tɔləreit] *ertragen*
human F ['hjuːmən] *Mensch*
suffer ['sʌfə] *leiden, gestatten*
bear [bɛə] *ertragen*
grizzled ['grizld] *grauhaarig*
muzzle ['mʌzl] *Schnauze*
rheumy ['ruːmi] *triefend*
confidence ['kɔnfidəns] *Vertrauen*
decision [di'siʒən] *Entscheidung*
momentous [mou'mentəs] *bedeutsam*

The dog would sit patiently for an hour at a time looking up at him.

question between the river and the house, would be all right, perfectly satisfactory in every way to dogs and men.

One very rainy summer, our old friend in a burst of confidence disclosed the wish of his heart. It was that he might be suffered to go down once more to Fowey in Cornwall, where he had been born, but had not been for fifty years. By some means or other the money was procured for this enterprise, and he was enabled to set off by excursion train for a fortnight's holiday. He was observed the day before his start talking at great length to the dog, and feeding it out of a paper-bag with caraway-seed biscuits. A letter was received from him during his absence; it was full of an almost passionate description of a regatta, of a certain "Joe Petherick" who had remembered him, of the "luvly weather" and other sources of his great happiness. On the fiftheenth day he was back at his corner seated on his box in the pouring rain, saying that he was "a different man, ten years younger, and ready to 'go' now, any day". But only four days later, the sun being for once in the heavens, he was so long in answering a salutation that we feared he had been visited by some kind of stroke; his old face had lost colour, it seemed stiff, and his eyes had almost disappeared.

Inquiry elicited from him the information that he was better than he had been, but that the dog was dead. They had put it away while he had

satisfactory [sætis'fæktəri] *befriedigend*
burst [bəːst] *Anwandlung*
disclose [dis'klouz] *enthüllen*
Fowey [fɔi] *Ort an der Küste von Cornwall*
Cornwall ['kɔːnwəl] *englische Grafschaft*
by some means or other [miːnz] *irgendwie*
procure [prə'kjuə] *beschaffen*
enterprise ['entə'praiz] *Unternehmen*
enable [i'neibl] *ermöglichen*
excursion train [iks'kəːʃən] *Ferien-, Sonderzug*
a fortnight's holiday ['fɔːtnaits] *ein 14tägiger Urlaub*
at great length [leŋθ] *sehr ausführlich*
paper-bag ['peipə bæg] *Tüte*
caraway-seed ['kærəwei-siːd] *Kümmelkorn . . .*
biscuit ['biskit] *Keks*
absence ['æbsəns] *Abwesenheit*
passionate ['pæʃənit] *leidenschaftlich*
description [dis'kripʃən] *Beschreibung, Schilderung*
regatta [ri'gætə] *Regatta*
luvly = lovely
source [sɔːs] *Quelle*
for once *diesmal*
heavens *Pl.* ['hevnz] *Firmament*
salutation [sæljuː'teiʃən] *Gruß*
fear [fiə] *(be)fürchten*
visit ['vizit] *heimsuchen, befallen*
stroke [strouk] *Schlaganfall*
disappear [disə'piə] *verschwinden*
inquiry [in'kwaiəri] *Erkundigung*
elicit [i'lisit] *entlocken*
put away F *fortjagen*

been gone, and he was afraid that he should miss the "faithful old feller".

"He was very good to me," he said; "always came for a bit of bread or biscuit. And he was company to me; I never knew such a sensible creature." He seemed to think that the dog must have pined during his absence, and that this had accelerated his end by making his owners think he was more decrepit than he really was.

The death of the dog, and the cold damp autumn that year, told heavily on the old man, but it was not till mid November that he was noted one morning absent from his post. As he did not reappear his lodging was sought out.

It was in a humble street, but the house was neat und clean, and the landlady seemed a good, rough woman. She informed us that our old friend was laid up "with pleurisy and the gouty rheumatics"; that by right, of course, he ought to be in the infirmary, but she didn't like to turn him out. An awful independent old feller, not having a soul in the world to close his eyes, though she would never be surprised if he got up and went out tomorrow, he was that stubborn!

We went upstairs. The door of the back room at the top was open; and through it the sound of our old friend's voice could be heard:

"O Lord God, that took the dog from me, and gave me this here rheumatics, help me to keep a stiff and

be afraid [ə'freid] *(be-) fürchten*
miss [mis] *vermissen*
faithful ['feiθful] *treu*
bit [bit] *Stückchen*
be company to ['kʌmpəni] *j-m Gesellschaft leisten*
sensible ['sensəbl] *verständig*
creature ['kriːtʃə] *Geschöpf*
pine [pain] *sich grämen*
accelerate [æk'seləreit] *beschleunigen*
owner ['ounə] *Besitzer*
decrepit [di'krepit] *altersschwach*
damp [dæmp] *feucht*
tell on *sich auswirken auf*
not till *erst*

note [nout] *bemerken*
absent ['æbsənt] *abwesend*
reappear ['riːə'piə] *wieder erscheinen*
lodgings *Pl.* ['lɔdʒiŋz] *Unterkunft, Zimmer*
sought out [sɔːt] *aufgesucht*
humble ['hʌmbl] *ärmlich*
neat [niːt] *ordentlich*
landlady ['lænleidi] *Wirtin*
rough [rʌf] *barsch*
be laid up F [leid] *bettlägerig sein*
pleurisy ['pluərisi] *Rippenfellentzündung*
gouty ['gauti] *gichtisch*
rheumatics F *Pl.* [ruː'mætiks] *Rheuma*
by right *eigentlich*
ought to *sollte (eigentlich)*
infirmary [in'fəːməri] *Krankenhaus*
turn out *hinausjagen*
awful F ['ɔːful] *schrecklich*
independent [indi'pendənt] *alleinstehend*
surprise [sə'praiz] *überraschen*
stubborn ['stʌbən] *eigenwillig, zäh*

contrite heart. I am an old man, O Lord God, and I am not one to go into that place. So God give me a stiff heart, and I will remember you in my prayers, for that's about all I can do now. I have been a good one in my time, O Lord, and cannot remember doing harm to any man for a long while now; so, good Lord, remember and do not forget me, now that I am down, and the rent going on. For ever and ever, Amen."

We allowed a little time to pass before we went in, unwilling that he should think we had overheard that prayer. He was lying in a small dingy bed, with a medicine bottle and glass beside him on an old trunk. There was no fire.

He was—it seemed—better than he had been; the doctor's stuff was doing him good.

Certain arrangements were made for his benefit, and in less than three weeks he was back again at his corner.

In the spring of the following year we went abroad and were absent several months. He was no longer at his post when at last we came back, and a policeman informed us that he had not been there for some weeks. We made a second pilgrimage to his lodgings.

The house had changed hands. The new landlady was a thin, anxious-looking young woman. Yes, the old man had been taken very ill—double pneumonia and heart disease, she thought. Anyway, she couldn't have the worry and responsibility of him,

upstairs ['ʌp'stɛəz] *nach oben, die Treppe hinauf*
contrite ['kɔntrait] *reuevoll*
stiff [stif] *fest*

---

remember [ri'membə] *eingedenk sein*
prayer [prɛə] *Gebet*
do harm to s. b. [hɑːm] *j-m Böses tun*
while [wail] *Weile, Zeit*
down [daun] *krank, elend*
rent [rent] *Miete*
pass [pɑːs] *vorübergehen*
(be) unwilling ['ʌn'wiliŋ] *nicht wollen*
overheard [ouvə'həːd] *belauscht*
dingy ['dindʒi] *schmutzig*
trunk [trʌŋk] *Truhe*
stuff F [stʌf] *„Zeug"*
arrangements [ə'reindʒmənt] *Vorkehrungen*
benefit ['benifit] *Erleichterung*
abroad [ə'brɔːd] *ins Ausland*
several ['sevrəl] *mehrere*
pilgrimage ['pilgrimidʒ] *Wallfahrt*
change hands *den Besitzer wechseln*
anxious ['æŋkʃəs] *ängstlich*
double ['dʌbl] *doppelseitig*
pneumonia [njuː'mounjə] Lungenentzündung
heart disease ['hɑːt di'ziːz] *Herzkrankheit*
anyway ['eniwei] *jedenfalls*
worry ['wʌri] *Ärger, Aufregung*
responsibility [rispɔnsə'biliti] *Verantwortung*

let alone her rent. She had had the doctor, and had him taken off. Yes, it had upset him a bit; he would never have gone if he'd had his choice; but of course she had her living to get. She had his bits of things locked up all right; he owed her a little rent. In her opinion he'd never come out again. She was very sorry for him, too, he'd given no trouble till he was taken ill.

Following up her information we repaired with heavy hearts to the house, which he had so often declared he would never enter. Having ascertained the number of his ward we mounted the beautifully clean stairs. In the fifth of a row of beds, our old friend was lying, apparently asleep. But watching him carefully, we saw that his lips, deep sunk between his frosty moustache and beard, were continually moving.

"He's not asleep," said the nurse; "he'll lie like that all the time. He frets."

At the sound of his name, he had opened his eyes, which, though paler and smaller and more rheumy, were still almost bright. He fixed them on us with a peculiar stare, as much as to say: "You've taken an advantage of me, finding me here." We could hardly bear that look, and hurriedly asked him how he was.

He tried to raise himself and answered huskily that he was better than he had been. We begged him not to exert himself, and told him how it was that we had been away, and so forth. He seemed to pay no

let alone *abgesehen von*
have s. b. taken off *j-n fortbringen lassen*
upset [ʌpˈset] *aus der Fassung bringen*
bits of things *Pl. Habseligkeiten*
lock up [lɔk] *einschließen*
owe [ou] *schulden*
opinion [əˈpinjən] *Meinung*
be sorry for s. b. *Mitleid haben mit j-m*
give trouble [ˈtrʌbl] *zur Last fallen*
be taken ill *krank werden*
follow up [ˈfɔlou] *weiter verfolgen*
repair [riˈpɛə] *sich begeben*
declare [diˈklɛə] *erklären*
ascertain [æsəˈtein] *ermitteln*
ward [wɔːd] *Station (Krankenhaus)*
mount [maunt] *hinaufsteigen*
beautiful [ˈbjuːtəful] *bewundernswert*
stairs *Pl.* [stɛəz] *Treppe(nhaus)*
row [rou] *Reihe*
apparent [əˈpɛərənt] *offenbar*
frosty [frɔsti] *ergraut*
moustache [məsˈtɑːʃ] *Schnurrbart*
nurse [nəːs] *Krankenschwester*
fret [fret] *sich grämen*
sound [saund] *Klang*
pale [peil] *bleich*
bright [brait] *strahlend*
peculiar [piˈkjuːljə] *eigentümlich*
stare [stɛə] *starrer Blick*
as much as to say *wie wenn er sagen wollte*
take advantage of s. b. [ədˈvɑːntidʒ] *j-n übervorteilen*
hurried [ˈhʌrid] *schnell*
husky [ˈhʌski] *heiser*
exert o. s. [igˈzəːt] *sich anstrengen*
and so forth [fɔːθ] *und so weiter*

attention, but suddenly said: "I'm in here; I don't mean to stay, I'll be going out in a day or two." We tried to confirm that theory, but the expression of his eyes seemed to take away our power of comfort, and make us ashamed of looking at him. He beckoned us closer.

"If I'd a-had the use of my legs," he whispered, "they'd never have had me. I'd a-gone in the river first. But I don't mean to stay – I'm going back home."

The nurse told us, however, that this was out of the question; he was still very ill.

Four days later we went again to see him. He was no longer there. He had gone home. They had buried him that morning.

pay attention [ə'tenʃən] *aufmerksam sein*
mean [mi:n] *beabsichtigen*
confirm [kən'fə:m] *bestätigen*
theory ['θiəri] *hier: Meinung*
expression [iks'preʃən] *Ausdruck*
comfort ['kʌmfət] *Trost*
ashamed [ə'ʃeimd] *beschämt*
beckon ['bekən] *winken*
I'd a-had = I should have had
I'd a-gone = I should have gone
be out of the question ['kwestʃən] *nicht in Frage kommen*
still [still] *noch*
go to see s. b. *j-n besuchen*
bury ['beri] *begraben*

(From: Quality and Other Stories. London, W. Heinemann.)

The Price

By W. L. George

When little Mrs. Van Roden found that her excellent maid must hasten to the bedside of a sick mother, she was annoyed. She did not show it, except by saying: "I suppose you will have to go." But she was in despair, for in the whole of her twenty years she had never been without nurse or maid. Her husband was not helpful.

"Get a temporary," he said.

"Don't be silly," said his wife. "Mason may be back in three days. I suppose I must ask one of the others."

Mrs. Van Roden found the others oddly reluctant. The parlourmaid said she supposed it could be managed; the head housemaid: "Of course, madam, if you want me to..." and there was about this "want" something fatal. At last the head housemaid said: "If you like, madam, there's Ellen. She sews well and . . ."

"Send Ellen," said Mrs. Van Roden, and Ellen soon appeared. She was hardly older than her mistress, not pretty, but fresh. She had sandy hair, blue eyes and a shy manner. The latter troubled Mrs. Van Roden. "She's timid," she thought. "Will probably be quite useless."

She was wrong. Within two days Mrs. Van Roden discovered that Ellen was born a lady's-maid, just as she might have been born a poet.

(house)maid [meid] *(Haus)Gehilfin*
hasten ['heisn] *eilen*
to the bedside ['bedsaid] *an das Krankenbett*
sick [sik] *krank*
be annoyed [ə'nɔid] *sich ärgern*
suppose [sə'pouz] *annehmen, vermuten*
despair [dis'pɛə] *Verzweiflung*
the whole of [houl] *die ganzen*
nurse [nəːs] *Kindermädchen*
husband ['hʌzbənd] *(Ehe)Mann*
helpful ['helpful] *behilflich*
temporary ['tempərəri] *vorübergehend(e Aushilfe)*
silly ['sili] *albern, dumm*
odd [ɔd] *merkwürdig*
reluctant [ri'lʌktənt] *widerstrebend, zögernd*
parlourmaid ['pɑːləmeid] *Stubenmädchen*
manage ['mænidʒ] *möglich machen, schaffen*
head [hed] *Ober . . ., erste*
of course [kɔːs] *natürlich*
fatal ['feitl] *unheilvoll*
sew [sou] *nähen*
appear [ə'piə] *erscheinen*
hardly ['hɑːdli] *kaum*
mistress ['mistris] *Herrin*
pretty ['priti] *hübsch*
sandy ['sændi] *strohblond*
shy [ʃai] *schüchtern*
manner ['mænə] *Auftreten, Verhalten*
trouble ['trʌbl] *beunruhigen*
timid ['timid] *schüchtern*
probable ['prɔbəbl] *wahrscheinlich*
useless ['juːslis] *unbrauchbar*
discover [dis'kʌvə] *entdecken*

Mason's three days were extended to a week. Her mother grew no better and no worse, and yet Mrs. Van Roden was happy. When after a month Mason wrote that she must stay at home Mrs. Van Roden contentedly told herself: "I've got Ellen."

Indeed she had Ellen, or something stronger than she had Ellen. The girl was happy. She had never thought of becoming a lady's-maid, and now her nature expanded in this predestined environment. She never had to be told anything twice, because she vibrated to the contacts and sights about her. For her it was not work but a continual delight to fold into tissue-paper the rustling silks, the brocades thick with silver and gold thread. She liked to polish the hairbrushes backed in silver, and above all she loved scent, the scent in the crystal bottle, the scent of the expensive soap. She was happy.

And so time passed. Mrs. Van Roden had at first intended to procure a maid, preferably French, but she was so surrounded by comfort that she put off the change, and, insensibly, Ellen passed from the housemaid to the lady's-maid. A year, two years, five years elapsed, and nothing disturbed the harmony of mistress and servant. Indeed, an unspoken affection formed between them; there was no reason why they should not spend their lives together. But this was not to happen: nine years after her promotion Ellen fell in love.

extend [iks'tend] *verlängern*
grew no better and no worse [gruː] *(ihr) ging es unverändert*
contented [kən'tentid] *zufrieden*
expand [iks'pænd] *sich entfalten*
predestine [priː'destin] *auserwählen*
environment [in'vaiərənmənt] *Umgebung*
vibrate [vai'breit] *zittern, beben*
continual [kən'tinjuəl] *beständig*
delight [di'lait] *Freude*
tissue-paper ['tisjuːpeipə] *Seidenpapier*
rustle ['rʌsl] *rascheln*
silk [silk] *Seide(nstoff)*
brocade [brə'keid] *Brokat(stoff)*
thread [θred] *Faden*
polish ['pɔliʃ] *putzen*
hairbrush ['hɛəbrʌʃ] *Haarbürste*
back [bæk] *einfassen*
scent [sent] *Duft, Wohlgeruch*
crystal ['kristl] *Kristall*
expensive [iks'pensiv] *teuer, kostbar*
intend [in'tend] *beabsichtigen*
procure [prə'kjuə] *sich besorgen*
preferably ['prefərəbli] *vorzugsweise*
surround [sə'raund] *umgeben*
put off *aufschieben*
change [tʃeindʒ] *Wechsel*
insensible [in'sensəbl] *unmerklich*
elapse [i'læps] *vergehen*
disturb [dis'təːb] *stören*
servant ['səːvənt] *Dienstmädchen, -bote*
affection [ə'fekʃən] *Zuneigung*
form [fɔːm] *entstehen*
reason ['riːzn] *Grund*
spend [spend] *verbringen*
happen ['hæpən] *geschehen*
promotion [prə'mouʃən] *Beförderung*

Mrs. Van Roden was surprised as well as shaken when Ellen announced that she was engaged and wanted to leave to get married. Ellen was thirty-two. She was not pretty, and yet in the eyes of one man she was beautiful.

It had happened quite quickly. Mr. Van Roden had a taste for new appliances, which made him buy an improved kind of electric heater. It arrived out of order; it was put right and went out of order again on the third, fifth, tenth, and fourteenth day of its existence, after which its owner trampled it to pieces. But meanwhile an electrician, while repairing the heater, had perceived the charm of Ellen. He was thirty-five and earned good wages.

"I don't know what I shall do without you," said Mr. Van Roden. "Still, I wish you every happiness."

So Ellen was married and she was very happy, happy in her husband and in the second year happy in her little girl, whom she called Flora after Mrs. Van Roden. Only one trifle now and then shook her serenity. Though Jim was well-paid, her surroundings had changed. Her sheets were coarse, her table-cloths without gloss, and her scent somewhat not the same. When Flora was born she wanted for her lace and fine lawn, and she knew that she could not have them. She reproached herself for these thoughts, but love her husband and child as she might, she could not drive them away.

fall in love *sich verlieben*

---

surprise [sə'praiz] *überraschen*
shaken ['ʃeikən] *erschüttert*
announce [ə'nauns] *verkünden*
engage [in'geidʒ] *sich verloben*
get married ['mærid] *(sich ver)heiraten*
taste [teist] *Vorliebe*
appliance [ə'plaiəns] *Gerät*
improve [im'pruːv] *verbessern*
heater ['hiːtə] *Heizofen*
put right *in Ordnung bringen*
owner ['ounə] *Besitzer*
trample ['træmpl] *(zer-)trampeln*
meanwhile ['miːn'wail] *inzwischen*
electrician [ilek'triʃən] *Elektriker*
perceive [pə'siːv] *bemerken*
charm [tʃaːm] *Reiz*
earn [əːn] *verdienen*
wages *Pl.* [weidʒiz] *Lohn*
still *dennoch*

trifle ['traifl] *Kleinigkeit*
shook [ʃuk] *erschütterte*
serenity [si'reniti] *heitere Ruhe*
well-paid ['wel'peid] *gutbezahlt*
surroundings *Pl.* [sə'raundiŋz] *Umgebung, -welt*
change [tʃeindʒ] *sich verändern*
sheet [ʃiːt] *Bettuch*
coarse [kɔːs] *grob*
table-cloth ['teiblklɔθ] *Tischtuch*
gloss [glɔs] *Glanz*
lace [leis] *Spitze*
lawn [lɔːn] *Batist*
reproach [ri'proutʃ] *Vorwürfe machen*
thought [θɔːt] *Gedanke*
love . . . as she might *so sehr sie . . . auch liebte*

When Flora was six months old Jim was knocked down by a motor-car as he crossed the street, and in a few minutes the brief episode of Ellen's married life was at an end. For the first days she did not face the consequences. She could only weep, only pace the two rooms where she had been so happy, holding to her breast the child that could not console her, that could not even understand. Her aunt, Mrs. Roberts, came to see her with her cousins, Minnie and Dorothy, and asked what she intended to do. Ellen could only cry, and at last her aunt went away.

However, after a week, when Ellen began to grow used to solitude, it came to her that she must do something, that she and Flora must live. Her husband had left behind him enough money to keep them a month. She had a month and for many days she brooded absurd plans; she would open a shop, become an insurance agent, go on the stage. What she meant, though she never expressed it, was that she would not part with Flora.

But she knew quite well that she must part with Flora. She was fit for only one trade, and she could not take Flora with her, so dominating her pride she went to Mrs. Roberts.

"Take her? Of course I'll take her, and bring her up like one of my own."

Ellen hesitated. Her aunt could have said nothing more likely to wound Ellen. She looked at her, red and gross, at the dirty table-cloth,

knock down [nɔk] *überfahren*
cross [krɔs] *überqueren*
brief [bri:f] *kurz*
episode ['episoud] *Zwischenspiel*
married life ['mærid] *Ehe*
face [feis] *ins Gesicht sehen, sich klarmachen*
consequence ['kɔnsikwəns] *Folge*
weep [wi:p] *weinen*
pace [peis] *hin- und hergehen (in)*
console [kən'soul] *trösten*
come to see *besuchen*
cousin ['kʌzn] *Kusine*
intend [in'tend] *beabsichtigen*
cry [krai] *weinen*
grow used to [ju:st] *sich gewöhnen an*
solitude ['sɔlitju:d] *Einsamkeit*
it came to her *es fiel ihr ein*
keep [ki:p] *(unt)erhalten, durchbringen*
brood [bru:d] *ausbrüten*
absurd [əb'sə:d] *unsinnig*
insurance [in'ʃuərəns] *Versicherung(s ...)*
part with [pa:t] *sich trennen von*
fit [fit] *geeignet, fähig*
trade [treid] *Beruf*
dominate ['dɔmineit] *beherrschen*
pride [praid] *Stolz*
like one of my own *wie mein eigenes*
hesitate ['heziteit] *zögern*
likely ['laikli] *geeignet*
wound [wu:nd] *verletzen*
gross [grɔs] *feist, plump*

the hideous vases on the chiffonier. She glanced at Minnie and Dorothy, at their badly curled hair, at a blouse where a button was replaced by a safety-pin; she saw Flora growing up in this atmosphere, not at all unkind, but thick with the air of the kitchen, enriched by cheap pleasure. And she had hoped ... fool! Her aunt said the last word on her folly when she unpacked the child's frocks.

"You spend too much, my girl," she said. "A good piece of flannelette is all people like you and me can afford."

She was right and Ellen knew it as she went away, but all the same she cried. Yet life was being made as easy as possible for Ellen. When she knew that she must once again serve in the house of another, she went to Mrs. Van Roden and asked for her recommendation.

"I can do better than that," said Mrs. Van Roden, laughing. "In two years I've had three maids. I've kept this one only because I'm afraid the next might be worse, though that's not likely. If you'll come back to me, Ellen, you'll be doing me a charity."

So Ellen came back. It was odd to return to the same house, to the same ornaments, the same work. After a while it seemed to her that her married life had been a happy dream, that she had gone right on from the nine years as Mrs. Van Roden's maid. And she was almost happy, for she had regained the surroundings natural to her; she had escaped poverty and

hideous ['hidiəs] *abscheulich, scheußlich*
chiffonier [ʃifə'niə] *Chiffonière, Schränkchen mit Schubfächern*
glance [glɑːns] *blicken*
curl [kəːl] *locken, kräuseln*
blouse [blauz] *Bluse*
replace [ri'pleis] ersetzen
safety-pin ['seiftipin] *Sicherheitsnadel*
grow up [grou] *aufwachsen*
atmosphere ['ætməsfiə] *Atmosphäre, Umgebung*
unkind [ʌn'kaind] *unfreundlich*
enrich [in'ritʃ] *bereichern*
cheap [tʃiːp] *billig*
fool [fuːl] *Närrin*
folly [fɔli] *Torheit*
unpack ['ʌn'pæk] *auspacken*
frock [frɔk] *Kleidchen*
spend [spend] *ausgeben*
flannelette [flænl'et] *Baumwollflanell*
afford [ə'fɔːd] *erschwingen, sich leisten*
all the same [seim] *trotzdem*
yet [jet] *jedoch*
possible ['pɔsibl] *möglich*
serve [səːv] *dienen*
recommendation [rekəmen'deiʃən] *Empfehlung*
keep [kiːp] *(be)halten*
be afraid [ə'freid] *sich fürchten*
worse [wəːs] *schlechter*
likely [laikli] *wahrscheinlich*
charity ['tʃæriti] *hier: großer Dienst*
ornament ['ɔːnəmənt] *Ausstattung, Luxus*
regain [ri'gein] *wiedergewinnen*
escape [is'keip] *entrinnen*
poverty ['pɔvəti] *Armut*

settled down in luxury like a well-fed cat.

Only without Flora, Flora whom she visited twice a week. Flora was together her delight and her agony. The child was pretty, very healthy, and adored the mother who always came with a gift. Ellen found life worth-while when she went to Mrs. Roberts to play with Flora and hear the word "Mother". Only... she had known it from the beginning ... as time went on and Flora became first three and then four, Ellen suffered more from the rough household. Flora was not well kept, her hair was often unbrushed, and into her voice crept a vulgar intonation. For months her mother watched the child sink into grossness. She suffered all the time now. She could think of nothing else, and at night she tried to make plans. She wondered if she would go mad, until one day something relieved her mind, set her free.

She took Flora away from Mrs. Roberts and placed her in the family of a young doctor of refined nature, glad of the child's board. His wife was charming.

"Safe," thought Ellen, "safe."

And now she was entirely happy. While she enjoyed the delicate air of Mrs. Van Roden's home she could, month by month and year by year, watch Flora turn into first a well-mannered child and then into a gracious young lady. At the age of twelve Flora was sent to a good boarding-school, and her mother was heroic enough to forbear from visit-

settle down ['setl] *sich einrichten*
luxury ['lʌkʃəri] *Luxus*
well-fed ['wel'fed] *wohlgenährt*
visit ['vizit] *besuchen*
agony ['ægəni] *Qual*
healthy ['helθi] *gesund*
adore [ə'dɔː] *innig lieben*
gift [gift] *Geschenk*
worth-while ['wəːθ'wail] *lohnend, der Mühe wert*
suffer from ['sʌfə] *leiden unter, an*
rough [rʌf] *hier: ungepflegt*
unbrushed [ʌn'brʌʃd] *ungebürstet*
creep [kriːp] *sich einschleichen*
vulgar ['vʌlgə] *vulgär*
intonation [intou'neiʃən] *Tonfall, Ausdruck*
grossness ['grɔsnis] *Roheit, Unanständigkeit*
wonder ['wʌndə] *sich fragen*
go mad [mæd] *wahnsinnig werden*
relieve [ri'liːv] *erleichtern*
mind [maind] *Gemüt, Herz*
set free *befreien, erlösen*
place [pleis] *unterbringen*
refined [ri'faind] *kultiviert, gebildet*
board [bɔːd] *Kost-, Unterhaltsgeld*
charming ['tʃɑːmiŋ] *reizend, entzückend*
entire [in'taiə] *ganz, völlig*
enjoy [in'dʒɔi] *genießen*
delicate ['delikit] *fein*
air [ɛə] *Atmosphäre*
turn into *verwandeln in, erziehen zu*
well-mannered ['wel'mænəd] *wohlerzogen*
gracious ['greiʃəs] *anmutig*
boarding-school ['bɔːdiŋskuːl] *Internat(sschule)*
heroic [hi'rouik] *heldenhaft*

ing her. The child must not suffer, even if it was that of a servant. Flora must have her chance.

Mrs. Roberts, who was growing old, was angry and amazed. "Can't make out what you think you're doing, Ellen. What are you trying to do with the child? Want her to be a lady? You mark my words, all she'll do is to go wrong. People like you and me cannot afford . . . by the way, how do you afford to keep her at that school? What are your wages now?"

She had often asked that question in vain, but today Ellen replied: "Uncle Fred. He died eight years ago. He left me . . . well, enough to bring up Flora."

Mrs. Roberts said no more, and by degrees saw Ellen less often. She was hurt because Uncle Fred had left her nothing. Ellen was fond of her aunt and missed her, but she told herself that it was as well for Flora to start in life unhandicapped by a coarse family. And now Flora was really starting in life. At eighteen she left school, calm, well-spoken, fit for any circle. She went to college, where she came to know the right girls. Four years later she could write after her name the initials M. D. At the age of twenty-six two beacons were lit in Flora's life. She became house-physician in the local clinic for children, and she married one of the surgeons who visited there.

Then only did she succeed in persuading her mother to retire. Ellen was only fifty-nine, but she had failed

forbear [fɔːˈbɛə] *es unterlassen*

angry [ˈæŋgri] *ärgerlich*
amaze [əˈmeiz] *erstaunen, überraschen*
mark s.b.'s words *j-s Worte beachten*
go wrong [rɔŋ] *auf die schiefe Bahn geraten*
by the way *nebenbei, übrigens*
in vain [vein] *vergeblich*
reply [riˈplai] *erwidern*
. . . ago [əˈgou] *vor . . .*
bring up [briŋ] *auf-, erziehen*
by degrees *Pl.* [diˈgriːz] *nach und nach*
less often [ˈɔːfn] *seltener*
hurt [həːt] *verletzen*
be fond of [fɔnd] *gern haben*
unhandicapped [ˈʌnˈhændikæpt] *unbelastet*
coarse [kɔːs] *ungebildet*
calm [kaːm] *ruhig, gelassen*
well-spoken [ˈwelˈspoukən] *redegewandt*
circle [ˈsəːkl] *(Gesellschafts)Kreis*
college [ˈkɔlidʒ] *College, Hochschule*
come to know *kennenlernen*
initial [iˈniʃəl] *(Anfangs-)Buchstabe*
M. D. = doctor of medicine *Dr. med.*
beacon [ˈbiːkən] *Fanal*
lit [lit] *angezündet*
physician [fiˈziʃən] *Arzt, Ärztin*
local [ˈloukəl] *örtlich, am Ort*
surgeon [ˈsəːdʒən] *Chirurg*
visit [ˈvizit] *Visite machen*
only [ˈounli] *erst*
succeed in [səkˈsiːd] *gelingen*
retire [riˈtaiə] *sich zur Ruhe setzen*
fail [feil] *nachlassen*

in the last few years. She seemed without strength, as if exhausted by a long effort. She took the pension which Mrs. Van Roden offered her and settled in lodgings not far from her daughter's home. She would not shame her by sharing her roof.

Less than two months later, when Flora called on her mother and read out the evening paper, she cried out:

"Mother, listen! Oh, how dreadful!"

"What is it?"

"Mother, Mrs. Van Roden!"

"Not dead?" cried Ellen.

"No, worse," said Flora.

She read out the hideous story. Mrs. Van Roden was rich, but even rich women sometimes need money and do not like to ask their husbands for it, so she had taken to a jeweller her bracelet of square emeralds, demanding a high price. On examination it was found that fifteen of the thirty-two stones were imitation. The jeweller did not know Mrs. Van Roden, so had her arrested. She was released on heavy bail.

"Oh, how awful," said Flora. "Why did she do it?"

Ellen looked up, and said in a weak voice: "She didn't. Someone had to give you your chance, my child. I'll pay the price."

exhaust [ig'zɔːst] *erschöpfen*
effort ['efət] *Anstrengung*
pension ['penʃən] *Rente*
offer ['ɔfə] *anbieten*

shame [ʃeim] *j-m Schande machen*
share [ʃɛə] *teilen*
roof [ruːf] *Dach*
call on *besuchen*
read out [red] *las vor*
dreadful ['dredful] *furchtbar*

jeweller ['dʒuːələ] *Juwelier*
bracelet ['breislit] *Armband*
square ['skwɛə] *viereckig*
emerald ['emərəld] *Smaragd*
examination [igzæmi'neiʃən] *Prüfung, Untersuchung*
imitation [imi'teiʃən] *Imitation*
have s.b. arrested [ə'restid] *j-n verhaften lassen*
release [ri'liːs] *freilassen*
heavy bail [beil] *hohe Kaution, hohe Bürgschaft*
awful ['ɔːful] *furchtbar*
weak [wiːk] *schwach*
voice [vɔis] *Stimme*

(From: *Selected Short Stories*. London, Chapman & Hall.)

The Philanthropist

By W. Pett Ridge

The young man at the 'Dispatch' office was responsible for what may be termed the kick-off. In looking back, the town discovered that the whole incident had some resemblance to the football which took place on Saturday afternoon; the bustle, the excitement, and even the examples of rough play were similar.

"My name," said the visitor timidly, when he had gained admission to the editor's room, "is Neville."

"On the Grampian Hills," suggested the youth, "your father feeds his flocks, a frugal swain whose constant care–"

"Australia, to be exact," said the caller. "Perth, to be more precise. I am a native of this town, and consequently I feel I owe something to it. You, perhaps, may be able to indicate what that something should be."

"My dear sir," cried the 'Dispatch' young man, jumping up, "pray take a chair. Take the settee. Have a cigarette? Help yourself to a match. My name's Gainsford. Now, then!" With a great air of shrewdness. "Let us get all this clear. What, speaking roughly, is the limit to which you are willing to go?'

"Can't go beyond five thousand."

"Pounds?"

"Pounds, of course."

"Oh, my giddy aunt!"

philanthropist [fi'lænθrəpist] *Menschenfreund*
dispatch [dis'pætʃ] *Depesche (Zeitung)*
responsible [ris'pɔnsəbl] *verantwortlich*
term [təːm] *(be)nennen*
kick-off ['kik'ɔf] *Anstoß*
incident ['insidənt] *Vorfall*
resemblance [ri'zembləns] *Ähnlichkeit*
bustle ['bʌsl] *Getriebe*
excitement [ik'saitmənt] *Aufregung*
timid ['timid] *schüchtern*
gain admission [gein] *Zutritt erlangen*
editor ['editə] *Redakteur*
Grampian Hills ['græmpiən] *Gebirge in Schottland*
suggest [sə'dʒest] *meinen, anspielen auf*
flock [flɔk] *(Schaf)Herde*
frugal ['fruːgəl] *genügsam*
swain [swein] *Schäfer*
Perth [pəːθ] *Stadt in Westaustralien*
be a native of ['neitiv] *geboren sein in*
owe [ou] *verdanken*
indicate ['indikeit] *angeben*
pray [prei] *bitte*
settee [se'tiː] *Sofa*
help o. s. to *sich bedienen mit*
air [ɛə] *Miene, Ansehen*
shrewdness ['ʃruːdnis] *Schlauheit*
limit ['limit] *Grenze*
beyond [biː'jɔnd] *(dar-) über . . . hinaus*
my giddy aunt F ['gidi 'ɑːnt] *du meine Güte!*

The young man sat again at the table and began to take notes. He put questions, and these were answered readily and modestly. Fortune had been good to Mr. Neville; he made money in wool at a period when others failed. Twenty-two years he had been absent from England. Landing at Plymouth the day before, he, without going to London, as most of the passengers had done, travelled direct to his birthplace.

"And," said young Gainsford, writing swiftly, "you detect a number of changes. You are astonished at the progress that has been made, and you consider it speaks well for the whole-heartedness and the public spirit ever shown by leading men of our town."

"Haven't had much time to glance around yet."

"To you," still taking it down from his own dictation, "it seems almost like a dream to be reviewing the scene—" Here he turned, and consulted the index of a volume called 'Familiar Quotations'. " 'Review the scene. And summon from the shadowy past, the forms that once have been.' "

"That's one way of putting it," admitted Mr. Neville.

"In treading the familiar streets you can imagine yourself a boy again."

"Wouldn't say that," corrected the visitor. "I'm on the wrong side of forty."

take notes *Pl.* [nouts] *Notizen machen*
modest ['mɔdist] *bescheiden*
fortune ['fɔːtʃən] *Schicksal*
fail [feil] *Bankrott machen*
Plymouth ['plimәθ] *Hafenstadt in Südengland*
birthplace ['bәːθpleis] *Geburtsort*
swift [swift] *schnell*
detect [di'tekt] *entdecken*
change [tʃeindʒ] *Veränderung*
astonish [әs'tɔniʃ] *sich wundern*
progress ['prougres] *Fortschritt(e)*
consider [kәn'sidә] *denken, meinen*
speak well for *zugunsten von . . . sprechen*
whole-heartedness ['houl'hɑːtidnis] *Aufrichtigkeit, Ernst*
public spirit ['pʌblik 'spirit] *Gemeinsinn*
glance around [glɑːns] *sich umsehen*
take down *niederschreiben*
review [ri'vjuː] *hier: wiedersehen*
scene [siːn] *Schauplatz*
consult [kәn'sʌlt] *zu Rate ziehen*
index ['indeks] *Register*
volume ['vɔljum] *Band*
familiar quotations *Pl.* [fә'miljә kwou'teiʃәnz] *„geflügelte Worte"*
summon ['sʌmәn] *herauf-, herbeirufen*
shadowy ['ʃædoui] *schattig, dämmerig*
put *ausdrücken, sagen*
admit [әd'mit] *zugeben*
tread [tred] *betreten*
imagine o. s. [i'mædʒin] *sich vorkommen als*
on the wrong side of forty *über vierzig hinaus*

"Mr. Neville," said the 'Dispatch' youth, as he wrote, "is in the prime of life, and attributes his good health to moderation in food and beverage, and to those industrious habits which were fostered in early years. It may be added that during the long period, and in spite of the wide distance separating him from those early years, he has never for a moment forgotten old acquaintances. Not a day has passed but he has sent a silent message to friends at home. We have now to make known the intentions of Mr. Neville. He has chosen the 'Dispatch' to be his intermediary, and we have the gratification to state that he proposes–"

That's where you find the signals against you, lad," said Mr. Neville. "So far, it's all easy enough. The trouble begins here."

Gainsford crossed knees and stared at the windows reflectively.

"Art gallery," he said, with deference.

"Guess again!"

"Addition to cottage hospital."

"Go on trying."

"Drinking fountain with sculptured figures," said the youth. His powers of thought seemed to be giving out.

"Bah!" ejaculated Mr. Neville.

"Annuities for old–"

"Look here," interrupted the other. He hit the table with his walking-stick. "I don't pretend that my notion is to hide my light under a bushel. I know as well as you do that if I want publicity there must

youth [juːθ] *junger Mann*
prime [praim] *Blüte(zeit)*
attribute [əˈtribjuːt] *zuschreiben*
moderation [mɔdəˈreiʃən] *Mäßigkeit*
food and beverage [ˈbevəridʒ] *Essen und Trinken*
industrious [inˈdʌstriəs] *fleißig*
habit [ˈhæbit] *Gewohnheit*
foster [ˈfɔstə] *pflegen*
separate [ˈsepəreit] *trennen*
acquaintance [əˈkweintəns] *Bekannte(r)*
but *daß nicht*
silent [ˈsailənt] *stumm*
message [ˈmesidʒ] *Botschaft*
intermediary [intəˈmiːdjəri] *Vermittler*
gratification [grætifiˈkeiʃən] *Genugtuung*
state [steit] *feststellen*
propose [prəˈpouz] *beabsichtigen*
you find the signals *Pl.* against you [ˈsignlz] *Sie können nicht weiter*
trouble [ˈtrʌbl] *Ärger*
cross knees *Pl.* [niːz] *die Beine übereinanderschlagen*
reflective [riˈflektiv] *nachdenklich*
art gallery [ˈgæləri] *Kunstgalerie*
deference [ˈdefərəns] *Ehrerbietung*
addition [əˈdiʃən] *Erweiterung*
cottage [ˈkɔtidʒ] *Baracken-, Behelfs-*
fountain [ˈfauntin] *Brunnen*
sculpture [ˈskʌlptʃə] *meißeln*
power of thought [θɔːt] *Vorstellungskraft*
give out *sich erschöpfen*
ejaculate [iˈdʒækjuleit] *ausstoßen*
annuity [əˈnjuːiti] *(Jahres)Rente*

be what you call a touch of the eccentric in the plan. Something that'll catch the eye, the ear, the head, and the heart."

There was silence for a few moments. Then young Gainsford raised his voice with the air of one suddenly inspired.

"Twenty pounds a year," he announced, "to ten spinster ladies, born in the town, who, having reached the age of thirty-five, are in but moderate circumstances."

"Could you make it widows?" asked Mr. Neville. "And of good appearance? I'm a bachelor myself, and I've always had a sympathy—"

"Make it widows," said the other handsomely. "And of good appearance." Mr. Neville took off his right glove, and there was the fervent gripping of hands which indicates complete and emphatic agreement. The notes, finished, were handed to the master printer to be set up.

They lunched at the Queen's Head, where a market ordinary was being held, and a flagon of Australian wine was ordered; at the first glass young Gainsford asked to be allowed to state that he was not, as might have been assumed, the proprietor and editor of the journal, but just a sub placed in charge in the temporary absence of the proprietor and editor. Demanding confidence, he begged that Mr. Neville would tell him if the offer might be regarded as genuine, and, on this, documents were submitted which removed all suspicions; moreover, Mr. Neville was able to

interrupt [intə'rʌpt] *unterbrechen*
hit [hit] *schlug auf*
pretend [pri'tend] *so tun als ob*
notion ['nouʃən] *Absicht*
hide [haid] *verbergen*
bushel ['buʃl] *Scheffel*
publicity [pʌb'lisiti] *Reklame*

---

touch [tʌtʃ] *Anflug*
eccentric [ik'sentrik] *überspannt*
silence ['sailəns] *Schweigen*
raise [reiz] *erheben*
inspire [in'spaiə] *inspirieren*
announce [ə'nauns] *verkünden*
spinster ['spinstə] *unverheiratet(e Frau)*
moderate ['mɔdərit] *bescheiden*
circumstances *Pl.* ['səːkəmstənsiz] *Verhältnisse*
widow ['widou] *Witwe*
bachelor ['bætʃələ] *Junggeselle*
appearance [ə'piərəns] *Erscheinung*
handsome ['hænsəm] *großzügig*
glove [glʌv] *Handschuh*
fervent ['fəːvənt] *innig*
gripping of hands ['gripiŋ] *Händedrücken*
emphatic [im'fætik] *ganz entschieden*
printer ['printə] *Drucker*
set up *setzen*
flagon ['flægən] *bauchige (Wein)Flasche*
assume [ə'sjuːm] *annehmen*
proprietor [prə'praiətə] *Inhaber*
sub F = subordinate *Angestellter*
place in charge [tʃɑːdʒ] *beauftragen*
temporary ['tempərəri] *vorübergehend*
offer ['ɔfə] *Angebot*
genuine ['dʒenjuin] *echt*

identify several of the men in the room, and one, coming over presently, recognized him. The grip of the hand that accompanied this induced Mr. Neville to turn to his journalist friend for help, and Gainsford explained that poor old Neville had been through rotten hard times, and could now be described, colloquially, as down and out. On this, the third party lost much of his enthusiasm, and saying casually, "Better days in store, perhaps", went back to his meal. The two, left alone, were in accord in deciding that, until the publication of the weekly issue of the newspaper, the whole matter had to be kept as a profound secret.

"I don't want a fuss," pleaded Mr. Neville. "Prematurely, that is to say. And these chaps here never used to think much of me, and I never thought too highly of them."

"Your interest, sir, is in the fair sex?"

"To a certain extent."

"May I ask how long you intend to remain with us?"

"I catch," he answered, "the last uptrain to London this evening."

The head-waiter approached with the extended arms of one about to give an effusing greeting. "Take me away," urged Mr. Neville to his companion, "and hide me."

He was escorted to the house on the outskirts of the town where a bed-sitting-room had, on the instructions of the master printer, been rented for Gainsford a week earlier.

submit [səb'mit] *vorlegen*
remove [ri'muːv] *beseitigen*
suspicion [səs'piʃən] *Verdacht, Argwohn*

---

identify [ai'dentifai] *identifizieren*
presently ['prezntli] *sofort*
recognize ['rekəgnaiz] *wiedererkennen*
accompany [ə'kʌmpəni] *begleiten*
rotten *sl.* ['rɔtn] *hundsmiserabel*
colloquial [kə'loukwiəl] *umgangssprachlich*
down and out F *„restlos fertig"*
party ['pɑːti] *Gesprächsteilnehmer*
enthusiasm [in'θjuːziæzəm] *Begeisterung*
casual ['kæʒjuəl] *gleichgültig*
be in store [stɔː] *bevorstehen, auf j-n warten*
be in accord [ə'kɔːd] *sich einig sein*
publication [pʌbli'keiʃən] *Erscheinen*
issue ['isjuː] *Ausgabe*
profound [prə'faund] *vollkommen*
secret ['siːkrit] *Geheimnis*
fuss [fʌs] *„Wirbel", Aufheben*
plead [pliːd] *dringend bitten*
premature [premə'tjuə] *vorzeitig*
chap F [tʃæp] *Bursche*
the fair sex ['fɛə 'seks] *das schöne Geschlecht*
to a certain extent [iks'tent] *bis zu einem gewissen Grade*
intend [in'tend] *beabsichtigen*
uptrain ['ʌp'trein] *in die Stadt fahrender Zug*
head-waiter ['hedweitə] *Ober(kellner)*
approach [ə'proutʃ] *herankommen*
extend [iks'tend] *ausstrecken*
effusive [i'fjuːsiv] *überschwenglich*

Leaving him in charge of the excellent landlady, the youth prepared to hurry back to the office to resume control there. "Mrs. Hedderwick," he said, "give us tea for two at five o'clock sharp." The land-lady beamed expansively. "My friend won't mind being left alone until then. Mrs. Hedderwick said the gentleman had only to ring if anything was wanted.

Gainsford had not reached the main road ere the landlady, with suitable apologies, begged Mr. Neville to accompany her to the garden, and oblige her with an opinion on the hollyhocks growing there. A presentable woman, her manner was so ingratiating that the visitor from Australia complied after but a moment's hesitation, and five minutes later the two were in the summer-house, and Mrs. Hedderwick was giving an animated description of the last hours of her late husband. It seemed natural that in the course of this she should give way to tears, and it would have been strange if Mr. Neville had omitted to comfort her.

"'Marry again,'" she quoted pathetically. "Them were almost his last words. 'Marry again,' he says, 'soon as ever you like!'"

"And did you?"

"I've never," declared Mrs. Hedderwick, "plucked up the heart to so much as look at any other man." "Until now," she added coyly.

"Don't let me keep you from your housework."

urge [əːdʒ] *drängen*
hide [haid] *verstecken*
escort [is'kɔːt] *begleiten*
outskirts *Pl.* ['autskəːts] *Stadtrand*
instructions *Pl.* [in'strʌkʃənz] *Anweisung(en)*
rent [rent] *mieten*

---

charge [tʃɑːdʒ] *Obhut*
resume [ri'zjuːm] *wieder aufnehmen*
control [kən'troul] *Aufsicht, Leitung*
sharp [ʃɑːp] *pünktlich*
beam [biːm] *strahlen*
expansive [iks'pænsiv] *überschwenglich*
won't mind *hätte nichts dagegen*
ere [ɛə] *als schon*
suitable ['sjuːtəbl] *passend, angemessen*
apology [ə'pɔlədʒi] *Entschuldigung*
accompany [ə'kʌmpəni] *begleiten*
oblige [ə'blaidʒ] *e-n Gefallen tun*
opinion [ə'pinjən] *Meinung*
hollyhock ['hɔlihɔk] *Stockrose*
presentable [pri'zentəbl] *stattlich*
ingratiate [in'greiʃieit] *einschmeicheln*
comply [kəm'plai] *einwilligen*
but *nur*
hesitation [hezi'teiʃən] *Zögern*
summer-house ['sʌməhaus] *Gartenlaube*
animated ['ænimeitid] *lebendig*
late [leit] *verstorben*
give way to tears *Pl.* [tiəz] *in Tränen ausbrechen*
strange [streindʒ] *merkwürdig*
omit [ou'mit] *versäumen*
comfort ['kʌmfət] *trösten*
them V = these
declare [di'klɛə] *verkünden*

"It's all done and finished hours ago," she explained brightly. "I'm out and about before my neighbours have begun to open their eyes, and I set to it, and everything's all spick and span before midday." She went on inconsequently. "Hedderwick used to say I was made to live in one of the colonies."

"I shall be going back to Australia in the course of a few weeks."

"Wouldn't I love to be going back with you!" She put her hand over her mouth in a girlish way, as though to restrain further speech of an unconsidered nature. An imitation of a postman's knock came from the distant front door, and Mrs. Hedderwick took the opportunity to absent herself.

She returned bearing two unstamped letters addressed to—Neville, Esq., and tidied the furniture of the summer-house to give him an opportunity of reading the contents. He did not speak, and the moment came when she was no longer able to suppress curiosity.

"People have soon found out where you are," she remarked.

"Can't understand how."

"There isn't much goes on in this town that doesn't get known pretty soon. You look quite red and confused, Mr. Neville."

"And so would anybody," he retorted, with spirit, "under the circumstances." He threw the notes on the wooden table, and Mrs. Hedder-

pluck up the heart *den Mut fassen*
coy [kɔi] *schüchtern*

---

explain [iks'plein] *erklären*
bright [brait] *strahlend*
out and about *mit allem fertig*
set to *sich daran machen*
spick and span ['spik ənd 'spæn] *blitzsauber*
inconsequent [in'kɔnsikwənt] *unlogisch*
colony ['kɔləni] *Kolonie*
girlish ['gəːliʃ] *mädchenhaft*
as though [ðou] *als ob*
restrain [ris'trein] *unterdrücken*
of an unconsidered nature ['ʌnkən'sidəd] *unbedacht*
imitation [imi'teiʃən] *Nachahmung*
distant ['distənt] *weit entfernt*
front door ['frʌnt 'dɔː] *Haustür*
opportunity [ɔpə'tjuːniti] *Gelegenheit*
absent o. s. [æb'sent] *sich entfernen*
bear [bεə] *tragen*
unstamped ['ʌn'stæmpt] *unfrankiert*
tidy ['taidi] *saubermachen, aufräumen*
furniture ['fəːnitʃə] *Möbel Pl.*
suppress [sə'pres] *unterdrücken*
curiosity [kjuəri'ɔsiti] *Neugier*
goes on *was vorgeht*
confused [kən'fjuːzd *verwirrt*
retort [ri'tɔːt] *erwidern*
spirit ['spirit] *gehobene Stimmung, gute Laune*
circumstance ['səːkəmstəns] *Umstand*
note [nout] *(Brief)Blatt*

wick assumed that he intended her to peruse them.

"How ever widow women can be so unmaidenly," she declared in shocked tones, "beats me. And knowing these two parties by sight, as I do, I can assure you, Mr. Neville, that you could never be happy with either of them."

"There's someone climbing over your fence," he pointed out.

A stout lady, with the aid of a creaking chair supplied by a neighbour, was trying to decide whether to make a sporting effort and jump into Mrs. Hedderwick's garden, or whether to trust the fates and tumble into it.

"How dare you!" cried Mrs. Hedderwick.

"Lend me a hand," begged the stout lady.

"I'll lend you nothing."

"You're a selfish-minded woman, Mrs. Hedderwick."

"Go back to your own home."

The fence gave way, and Mr. Neville, watching the scene from the doorway of the summer-house, felt certain he was not seeing either lady at her best. Excuses for them could be imagined. Mrs. Hedderwick had to face a damage to property; the other was likely enough suffering from bruises. Mrs. Hedderwick, the first to regain composure, turned to him.

"This is no sight for you, sir," she declared. "Come indoors."

assume [ə'sjuːm] *annehmen*
peruse [pə'ruːz] *durchlesen*
unmaidenly ['ʌn'meidnli] *unmädchenhaft*
in shocked tones *Pl.* [tounz] *entrüstet*
(that) beats me F *(das) kapiere ich nicht*
assure [ə'ʃuə] *versichern*
climb [klaim] *klettern*
fence [fens] *Zaun*
stout [staut] *beleibt, stämmig*
aid [eid] *Hilfe*
creak [kriːk] *knarren*
supply [sə'plai] *beschaffen*
decide [di'said] *sich entscheiden*
sporting [spɔːtiŋ] *sportlich*
effort ['efət] *Anstrengung*
trust [trʌst] *vertrauen*
fates *Pl.* [feits] *Schicksalsgöttinnen*
tumble ['tʌmbl] *purzeln*
how dare you [dɛə] *wie können Sie es wagen*
lend a hand *helfen*
selfish-minded ['selfiʃ-'maindid] *selbstsüchtig*
give way *nachgeben*
doorway ['dɔːwei] *Tür, Eingang*
either ['aiðə] *jeder von beiden*
at one's best *von der besten Seite*
imagine [i'mædʒin] *sich denken*
face [feis] *sich gegenüber sehen*
damage ['dæmidʒ] *(Be-) Schädigung*
property ['prɔpəti] *Eigentum, Besitz*
likely ['laikli] *wahrscheinlich*
bruise [bruːz] *Quetschung*
regain [ri'gein] *wiedererlangen*
composure [kəm'pouʒə] *Fassung, Haltung*

"You pretty beauty, you," screamed the corpulent lady. It seemed clear there was no intention of offering a compliment.

In the house, Mrs. Hedderwick took the line of frankness. The master printer at the 'Dispatch' offices was her brother-in-law, and he had acted in the interests of the family by acquainting her promptly with Mr. Neville's intentions; she had thought as, apparently, others had considered, that an improvement could be made in them. "And if you do get any idea of taking a wife back with you," urged Mrs. Hedderwick earnestly, "I hope you'll remember that I was the first in the field." Not without symptoms of alarm, he called her attention to the fact that six ladies were waiting in an orderly queue at the front railings. She went out at once, and opened the tradesmen's gate at the side of the house.

"This way," she said amiably, "all who want a talk with Mr. Neville." As the last filed through, she signalled to him, and he made his escape.

Young Gainsford, in shirt-sleeves at the 'Dispatch' office, put tasks away, and listened to the account given. When Mr. Neville spoke with a certain admiration of Mrs. Hedderwick the youth shook his head.

"She's the best landlady in the town," he said firmly. "I can't spare her."

"Is there time, then, to make some alteration in the paragraph?"

pretty beauty ['bjuːti] *„nette Person"*
intention [in'tenʃən] *Absicht*
offer ['ɔfə] *vorbringen, äußern*
take the line of frankness ['fræŋknis] *offen, freimütig sein*
brother-in-law ['brʌðərinlɔː] *Schwager*
acquaint [ə'kweint] *bekannt machen*
apparent [ə'pærənt] *offenbar*
consider [kən'sidə] *erwägen*
improvement [im'pruːvmənt] *Verbesserung*
urge [əːdʒ] *eindringlich vorstellen*
alarm [ə'lɑːm] *Bestürzung*
orderly ['ɔːdəli] *wohl geordnet*
queue [kjuː] *Reihe, Schlange*
railings *Pl.* ['reiliŋz] *Geländer, Zaun*
tradesmen's gate ['treidzmənz] *Lieferanteneingang*
amiable ['eimjəbl] *liebenswürdig*
file [fail] *hintereinander marschieren*
signal ['signl] *(ein) Zeichen geben*
make one's escape [is'keip] *fliehen, entkommen*
shirt-sleeve ['ʃəːtsliːv] *Hemdsärmel*
tasks *Pl.* [tɑːsks] *Aufgaben, Arbeit*
account [ə'kaunt] *Bericht*
admiration [ædmə'reiʃən] *Bewunderung*
firm [fəːm] *bestimmt*
spare [spɛə] *entbehren*
alteration [ɔːltə'reiʃən] *Änderung*
paragraph ['pærəgrɑːf] *(Zeitungs)Artikel*

"It is never too late to amend," said Gainsford, taking up the proofs. "And don't you wait about for the last train, my dear sir. I'll borrow a car and drive you to the junction. The fact is, you are not safe here!"

The Education Committee passed a vote of thanks at its next meeting. "Feeling that the great liberality shown by a former townsman will be deeply appreciated by the selected children on reaching the age of fourteen."

amend [ə'mend] *verbessern*
proof [pru:f] *Korrekturbogen*
borrow ['bɔrou] *leihen*
junction ['dʒʌŋkʃən] *Bahnstation*
education [edju:'keiʃən] *Erziehungs-, Schul-*
committee [kə'miti] *Ausschuß*
pass a vote of thanks [vout] *dafür stimmen, (den) Dank auszusprechen*
liberality [libə'ræliti] *Großzügigkeit*
townsman ['taunzmən] *Mitbürger*
appreciate [ə'pri:ʃieit] *schätzen, würdigen*
select [si'lekt] *auswählen*

(From: Leaps and Bounds, in: Humour of To-day. London, G. G. Harrap & Co.)

The Bad Eggs

By D. Newton

Related by Dr. Jaynes, Police Surgeon

"There's something queer about it," Paul Toft muttered, his seer's eyes brooding over the view. "Something... wicked."

"Nonsense," I said. "It's merely the granite. On a grey day like this, it gives even a lovely landscape a bleak tinge."

"All those heaped pyramids against the sky," he mooned on. "Like livid beasts, crouching to spring."

"They're only heaps of china-clay from the mines in the hills," I told him. Yet I knew what he meant.

Notching the whole skyline were the tall, white cones of the Cornish clay dumps. They seemed freakishly out of place in the scenery. More, their huge, blanched stillness gave one a sort of spiritual unease.

"I wonder if it's that," Toft mused, as I explained my feelings. "I don't think so. We've seen them for miles. This is new–I feel it."

"No," I cut him short," you don't– not on a holiday. All police work is definitely ruled out. Also, in the present condition of our feet, we'll not reach St. Frail by dinner-time unless we step lively."

Yet, oddly enough, we had not gone another twenty yards before I broke my own ruling by crying: "Here's a first-class mystery for you, anyhow. How did these three eggs get on to the road without breaking?"

bad egg [eg] *faules Ei; übler Kerl*
surgeon ['sə:dʒən] *Arzt*
queer [kwiə] *merkwürdig*
mutter ['mʌtə] *murmeln*
seer ['si:ə] *Prophet*
mere [miə] *bloß*
brood [bru:d] *grübeln*
wicked ['wikid] *böse*
bleak [bli:k] *öde, trübe*
tinge [tindʒ] *Färbung*
heap [hi:p] *aufhäufen*
moon [mu:n] *hier: träumen, phantasieren*
livid ['livid] *fahl*
crouch [krautʃ] *sich (nieder)ducken*
china-clay ['tʃainəklei] *Kaolin, Porzellanerde*
notch [nɔtʃ] *einschneiden*
skyline ['skailain] *Horizont*
cone [koun] *Kegel*
Cornish ['kɔ:niʃ] *kornisch, aus Cornwall*
dump [dʌmp] *Halde*
freakish ['fri:kiʃ] *grotesk*
out of place *fehl am Platz*
blanched [blɑ:ntʃd] *bleich*
stillness ['stilnis] *Stille, Ruhe*
spiritual ['spiritjuəl] *seelisch*
unease [ʌn'i:z] *Unbehagen*
muse [mju:z] *grübeln*
cut short *unterbrechen*
rule out [ru:l] *verbieten*
St. Frail [snt'freil] *erfundener Ortsname*
step lively ['laivli] *einen Schritt zulegen*
odd [ɔd] *seltsam*
yard [jɑ:d] *Yard (0,91 m)*
ruling ['ru:liŋ] *Entscheidung*
mystery ['mistəri] *Rätsel*

"Eggs?" Toft said, limping up. "Oh, from a farm cart. Dropped out!"

That wouldn't do at all, I pointed out. The road was granite hard, there wasn't even mud enough to break their fall, yet there those three hens' eggs were, right on the crown of the road, without as much as a crack in their shells.

"Odd—yes, most!" Toft's great domed head was bending in dreamy concentration over the miraculous eggs. "You're right, Jaynes. Something decidedly queer here."

"How the old war-horse pricks his ears at the mere hint of a mystery," I laughed. "Yet I think I can solve this one myself. See that patch of oil? A car stood on this spot for some time. Yes, and there's mud enough to show that something squarish was pressed hard on the macadam. That means a jack was used. A punctured tire was changed here. The jack was got from a locker under the seat. A basket of eggs standing on that seat naturally had to be lifted off and placed on the road. It tipped up and these three eggs rolled gently out. As they weren't seen it must have been night. Last night, probably, as they are clean and undamaged by traffic. Am I right?"

"That is exactly what happened," he nodded, as though he felt it all. "But that's not all. I feel—"

As he spoke a comic thing happened. He gently touched one of the eggs with his stick. It rolled against the others, and all exploded with small, sharp detonations. Thereupon

limp up [limp] *hinterherhinken; wiederholen*
farm cart [kɑːt] *Bauernwagen*
that wouldn't do at all *das würde es nicht erklären*
mud [mʌd] *Schlamm*
break their fall *ihren Fall dämpfen, abfangen*
right on the crown of the road [kraun] *mitten auf der Straße*
without as much as *nicht einmal mit*
crack [kræk] *Riß, Sprung*
shell [ʃel] *Schale*
domed [doumd] *gewölbt*
bend [bend] *sich beugen*
miraculous [mi'rækjuləs] *wunderbar*
decided [di'saidid] *entschieden*
war-horse F ['wɔːhɔːs] *Haudegen*
prick one's ears *Pl.* [prik] *die Ohren spitzen*
hint [hint] *Andeutung*
solve [sɔlv] *lösen*
patch [pætʃ] *Fleck*
spot [spɔt] *Stelle*
squarish ['skwɛəriʃ] *viereckig*
macadam [mə'kædəm] *Schotter*
jack [dʒæk] *Wagenheber*
puncture ['pʌŋktʃə] *platzen*
tire ['taiə] *Autoreifen*
locker ['lɔkə] Kasten
lift [lift] *hochheben*
place [pleis] *setzen, stellen*
tip up [tip] *umkippen*
gentle ['dʒentl] *langsam, sanft*
probable ['prɔbəbl] *wahrscheinlich*
undamaged ['ʌn'dæmidʒd] *unbeschädigt*
nod [nɔd] *nicken*

explode [iks'ploud] *zerplatzen (lassen)*
detonation [detou'neiʃən] *Knall*

there arose the most appalling stench that ever sickened man. It sent us scurrying out of range and also it ended the incident in laughter.

"Rotten eggs! Strange!" was all the old fellow muttered. "Too clean to have been there long, yet so old in decay that their own gases exploded them. Yes—I feel something wrong."

"The mere smell was proof enough for me," I scoffed.

The joke kept us going all the way to St. Frail, which was helpful, anyhow. We were on the second day only of a walking tour through Cornwall, visiting the little harbours and the lovely coves, and, in our first eagerness, had rather overdone things to the damage of our feet.

St. Frail proved an enchanting place. Deep, blue sea-ways winding between steep, stern hills. A tiny harbour set about with old buildings, such as dream pirates might people. From the lounge of our hotel on the hill, we looked down over a tight-packed mass of fantastic roofs into the glowing pool of the port. On the still mirror of the water, vessels of all sizes and shapes floated or moved with the silent grace of birds.

"Quite a lot of deep-sea craft, too," I commented. "There's a Spanish steamer alongside the railway quay. The one above her is a Dutchman, and, by Jove, this one going out is from the United States. Who'd have thought that a port like this—"

arise [ə'raiz] *sich erheben*
appalling [ə'pɔːliŋ] *entsetzlich*
stench [stentʃ] *Gestank*
sicken ['sikn] *anekeln*
send s. b. scurrying ['skʌriiŋ] *j-n fortjagen*
out of range [reindʒ] *außer Reichweite*
incident ['insidənt] *Vorfall*
laughter ['lɑːftə] *Gelächter*
rotten ['rɔtn] *(ver)faul(t)*
decay [di'kei] *Fäulnis*
gas [gæs] *Gas*
smell [smel] *Geruch*
proof [pruːf] *Beweis*
scoff [skɔf] *spotten*
joke [dʒouk] *Spaß*
keep going *hier: unterhalten*
anyhow ['enihau] *jedenfalls*
walking tour ['tuə] *Fußwanderung*
Cornwall ['kɔːnwəl] *englische Grafschaft*
cove [kouv] *kleine Bucht*
eagerness ['iːgənis] *Eifer*
rather [rɑːðə] *ziemlich*
overdo ['ouvədu] *übertreiben*
damage ['dæmidʒ] *Schaden*
enchanting [in'tʃɑːntiŋ] *entzückend*
steep [stiːp] *steil*
stern [stəːn] *düster*
tiny ['taini] *winzig*
people ['piːpl] *bevölkern, -wohnen*
lounge [laundʒ] *Halle, Foyer*
tight-packed ['tait'pækt] *dichtgedrängt*
pool [puːl] *Becken*
vessel ['vesl] *(Wasser-) Fahrzeug*
size [saiz] *Größe*
shape [ʃeip] *Form*
float [flout] *treiben*
grace [greis] *Würde*
deep-sea craft [krɑːft] *Hochseeschiff(e)*
comment ['kɔmənt] *bemerken*

"Stay up till four in the morning and you'll see a Jap come in," a sour voice from behind us broke in, and we turned to see a heavy, uncouth man lounging in a chair.

"That makes it even more remarkable," I said. "I never dreamed these little ports were so busy."

"Probably because you never heard of china-clay before in your life," the fellow grunted rudely. "Cornwall's having a little boom—shipping the stuff all over the world."

He spoke with a sneering petulance. He was a lumpy, powerful fellow, with heavy cheek-bones and an over-jowled face, which was made biscuit sallow by black hair. His dark spectacles could not hide the glitter of his eyes, which seemed very dark. He was slightly foreign, opinionated and thoroughly disagreeable.

"Are you in the china-clay trade?" I asked.

"I am not!" he rapped, as though I had insulted him. Yet he added, "It'd be better than hunting mares' nests, anyhow. Anything would be, in these holes. They look 'sweet' to trippers, I don't doubt," that was a jeer at us, "but give me a graveyard—there's more excitement there. Even the clay shipping is only a flea-bite—the rest's dead. See those two steamers buoy-anchored over there! They're laid up for lack of trade. So's the one abreast the quay. There are more up the cove. Cornwall's full of

quay [kiː] *Kai*
Dutchman [ˈdʌtʃmən] *Holländer*
by Jove [dʒouv] *Donnerwetter!*

Jap F [dʒæp] = Japanese
sour [ˈsauə] *mürrisch*
uncouth [ʌnˈkuːθ] *ungeschlacht, plump*
lounge [laundʒ] *sich rekeln, faulenzen*
grunt [grʌnt] *grunzen, brummen*
rude [ruːd] *grob, unverschämt*
boom [buːm] *Aufschwung*
stuff F [stʌf] *„Zeug"*
sneering [sniəriŋ] *höhnisch*
petulance [ˈpetjuləns] *Verdrießlichkeit*
lumpy [ˈlʌmpi] *plump*
cheek-bone [ˈtʃiːkboun] *Backenknochen*
over-jowled [ˈouvəˈdʒauld] *mit starkem Unterkiefer*
sallow [ˈsælou] *bläßlich*
spectacles *Pl.* [ˈspektəklz] *Brille*
glitter [ˈglitə] *Funkeln*
slightly [ˈslaitli] *leicht*
opinionated [əˈpinjəneitid] *starrsinnig*
thoroughly [ˈθʌrəli] *völlig, absolut*
disagreeable [disəˈgriəbl] *widerlich*
rap [ræp] *herauspoltern*
insult [inˈsʌlt] *beleidigen*
hunt [hʌnt] *jagen*
mare's nest [mɛəz] *unsinnige Entdeckung, Seeschlange*
hole [houl] *Höhle*
tripper [ˈtripə] *Ausflügler*
doubt [daut] *zweifeln*
jeer [dʒiə] *Spott, Hohn*
graveyard [ˈgreivjɑːd] *Friedhof*
flea-bite [ˈfliːbait] *Flohstich, Kleinigkeit*
buoy-anchored [ˈbɔiˈæŋkəd] *an der Boje verankert*

'em. Stagnation everywhere—and I've got to live in it."

"Hunting mares' nests?" Paul Toft put in dreamily. Our new acquaintance was glaring blackly at the reedy detective. I said jokingly: "My friend is naturally interested in mares' nests. He's a detective."

The effect of that was surprising. The man's mouth dropped open, and he said thickly with a curious blend of shock and fear: "What? Is Scotland Yard in this?"

I explained that Paul Toft was merely an officer of the provincial police force at Stripe, where I was also Medical Officer, and that we were on a walking holiday. Without another word, he left the lounge.

"A most unpleasant proposition, that chap," I said.

"Yes," Toft murmured. "Mixed up with the queerness about this place, too . . . Yes, I feel that . . ."

"Nothing savoury from the look of him, and nothing we're going to bother about on our holiday," I said, and ordered him to early bed.

Our feet being in a bad state next morning, we decided to have an easy day, and our waiter telling us that there was first-rate fishing in the creeks, which he called Pills, we agreed to spend a lazy day that way.

We had to pass the quay on our way to hire a boat, and we saw that, as our uncouth friend had promised, a Japanese vessel had taken the place of the Dutchman. Both this vessel and the Spaniard were being loaded

lay up *außer Dienst stellen, auflegen*
lack [læk] *Mangel*
abreast [ə'brest] *neben*

---

stagnation [stæg'neiʃən] *Stillstand, Flaute*
acquaintance [ə'kweintəns] *Bekannte(r)*
glare [glɛə] *starren*
reedy ['riːdi] *schlank*
joke [dʒouk] *scherzen*
surprising [sə'praiziŋ] *überraschend*
thickly ['θikli] *dumpf, mit belegter Stimme*
curious ['kjuəriəs] *merkwürdig*
blend [blend] *Mischung*
Scotland Yard ['skɔtlənd 'jɑːd] *(Sitz der) Londoner Kriminalpolizei*
Stripe [straip] *erfundener Ortsname*
medical officer ['medikəl] *Amtsarzt*
proposition F [prɔpə'ziʃən] *Individuum*
chap F [tʃæp] *Bursche*
mixed up [mikst] *zusammen*
queerness ['kwiənis] *Merkwürdigkeit*
savoury ['seivəri] *angenehm*
bother ['bɔðə] *sich aufregen*
order s. b. to early bed *j-n früh ins Bett schikken*
state [steit] *Zustand*
decide [di'said] *sich entscheiden*
waiter ['weitə] *Kellner, Ober*
first-rate ['fəːst'reit] *erstklassig*
creek [kriːk] *(kleine) Bucht*
lazy ['leizi] *faul*
hire ['haiə] *mieten*
promise ['prɔmis] *versprechen*
Spaniard ['spænjəd] *Spanier*
load [loud] *beladen; Ladung*

with clay, and we stopped to watch the work.

We saw whole railway trucks hoisted to the top of a tower and tipped over so that their loads of big white lumps poured down a chute. From this chute movable belt-conveyors were so arranged that each hold could be loaded in turn without the vessel being moved. In spite of the milky clouds of claydust that covered everything, we were fascinated by the neat celerity of the machinery, and forgot even our fishing until we saw our rude friend of the night before on the Japanese ship.

He appeared to have been making some sort of inspection, for a couple of other civilians were with him, while a small Japanese officer hovered behind them and bowed them off the gang-plank.

Our man looked sourer than ever and, when he saw us, not only broke into the blackest of scowls, but for a moment seemed as though he meant to come over and curse us for spying on him.

I found it all a matter of humour. "The mystery deepens," I chuckled. "Our questionable friend is caught trafficking with the inscrutable East ... Which, by Jove, solves the mystery of the eggs. They were Dragons' eggs–not hens'. Can't you see? The Dragon of the East–the Dragon of war–Japan's military activities in Manchuria. There's the answer to the riddle. The Japs are going to use rotten eggs as a new kind of poison gas!"

truck [trʌk] *Güterwagen*
hoist [hɔist] *hochheben, hieven*
tip over *überkippen*
lump [lʌmp] *Klumpen*
pour [pɔː] *hier: rollen, rutschen*
chute [ʃuːt] *Gleitbahn, Rutsche*
movable ['muːvəbl] *beweglich*
belt-conveyor ['beltkən'veiə] *Förderband*
hold [hould] *Laderaum*
in turn *der Reihe nach*
claydust ['kleidʌst] *Lehmstaub*
cover ['kʌvə] *bedecken*
fascinate ['fæsineit] *fesseln, bannen*
neat [niːt] *ordentlich*
celerity [si'leriti] *Geschwindigkeit*
appear [ə'piə] *scheinen*
inspection [in'spekʃən] *Kontrolle*
a couple of ['kʌpl] *ein paar*
civilian [si'viljən] *Zivilist*
hover ['hɔvə] *sich herumdrücken*
bow s. b. off [bau] *j-n unter Verbeugungen hinaus geleiten*
gang-plank ['gæŋplæŋk] *Laufplanke*
scowl [skaul] *finsteres Gesicht*
curse [kəːs] *verfluchen*
spy on [spai] *nachspionieren*
a matter of humour ['hjuːmə] *eine komische Sache*
chuckle [tʃʌkl] *kichern*
questionable ['kwestʃənəbl] *fragwürdig*
traffic ['træfik] *handeln, schachern*
inscrutable [in'skruːtəbl] *unergründlich*
dragon ['drægən] *Drache*
Japan [dʒə'pæn] *Japan*
Manchuria [mæn'tʃuəriə] *Mandschurei*
poison ['pɔizn] *Gift*

I laughed at my fantastic idea, and was considerably taken aback when Toft flashed on me that look of alertness that is the signal that something I have said has given a lead to his strange gifts.

"Queer, how even when you're joking, Doctor, there's something in you that helps," he said.

"Why, I was only fooling, man!" I gasped. "And how did I help? Do you feel these Japs are smuggling war materials?"

"I wonder?" he murmured, vague once more. "No-o." I can't say. Only I feel there's a link . . .

We spent a lazy and idyllic day. Not that we caught many fish, for, after eating the excellent lunch the hotel put up for us, we slept most of the afternoon.

That was unwise. When we awoke we found that what had been a wide expanse of water was now mainly mud—and we were high and dry on it. Not a soul came near to help us, we just had to sit in the boat until the tide came up to release us.

That happened just after nine, and as we were pretty hungry by then, I decided, being the better oarsman, it would be quicker if I did the rowing while Toft steered. I was, therefore, not at all pleased when he cried softly: "Oars in, Doctor," and, obeying, I found that we had overshot our landing place and were scraping the rusty plates of the steamer laid up abreast the railway quay.

considerable [kən'sidərəbl] *erheblich*
taken aback [ə'bæk] *bestürzt*
flash [flæʃ] *aufblitzen lassen*
alertness [ə'ləːtnis] *Wachsamkeit*
lead [liːd] *Hinweis, Wink*
strange [streindʒ] *seltsam*
gift [gift] *Gabe, Fähigkeit*
fool [fuːl] *zum Narren halten, Spaß machen*
gasp [gɑːsp] *keuchen*
smuggle ['smʌgl] *schmuggeln*
materials *Pl.* [mə'tiəriəlz] *Material, Ausrüstung*
vague [veig] *vage, unbestimmt*
link [liŋk] *(Binde)Glied*
idyllic [ai'dilik] *idyllisch*
caught [kɔːt] *fing*
excellent ['eksələnt] *vorzüglich*
put up *darbieten*
slept [slept] *schlief*
unwise ['ʌn'waiz] *unklug*
awoke [ə'wouk] *erwachten*
expanse [iks'pæns] *breite Fläche*
main [mein] *hauptsächlich*
dry [drai] *trocken*
tide [taid] *Flut*
release [ri'liːs] *befreien*
pretty ['priti] *ziemlich*
by then *inzwischen*
decide [di'said] *entscheiden*
oarsman ['ɔːzmən] *Ruderer*
row [rou] *rudern*
steer [stiə] *steuern*
please [pliːz] *erfreuen*
soft [sɔft] *leise*
oar [ɔː] *Ruder*
obey [ə'bei] *gehorchen*
overshot ['ouvə'ʃɔt] *über ... hinausgeschossen*
scrape [skreip] *schaben, kratzen*
rusty ['rʌsti] *rostig*
plate [pleit] *(Eisen)Platte*

About sixty feet away from us was the Japanese steamer, still being loaded by an overtime gang. A multitude of bright arc-lamps shone on and around her. That queer faculty of Toft, that had linked the mystery of the bad eggs with the East, had impelled him to select the deep shadows under this ship as an excellent vantage point to spy on the Jap.

I turned to ask what bee he had in his bonnet now, and got a shock.

He was not looking at the Jap. He had his back to her. Instead he was leaning over, his ear close up against the plates of the laid-up ship. He motioned me to listen, too, but though I strained my ears, I could hear nothing out of the way, save a faint strum of melody from the far interior of the vessel. Yet that, it seemed, was what he wanted. He asked me what I thought of it.

"Well, I've heard just that aimless sort of tune in an Arab café," I admitted.

"Eastern!" he nodded. "The East again, Doctor ... All right, we'll go ashore now."

We did not go there direct. Toft steered all round the laid-by vessel, studying her, but apart from learning that her name was the 'Diana Rea' she was lightless enough to be completely deserted. All the same, when we reached shore and were paying for our boat, Toft asked about this vessel.

"She's one o' Mr. Phillepi's junkships," the boatman told us, then seeing blankness in Toft's face: "You

foot [fut] *Fuß (0,3 m)*
overtime ['ouvətaim] *Überstunden*
gang [gæŋ] *Arbeitskolonne*
multitude ['mʌltitjuːd] *Menge*
arc-lamp ['ɑːklæmp] *Bogenlampe*
faculty ['fækəlti] *Fähigkeit*
link [liŋk] *verbinden*
impel [im'pel] *(an)treiben*
select [si'lekt] *auswählen*
vantage point ['vɑːntidʒ] *günstige Stelle*
spy on [spai] *nachspionieren*
have a bee in one's bonnet F ['bɔnit] *„einen Vogel haben"*
lean [liːn] *sich lehnen*
close up [klous] *ganz dicht*
motion ['mouʃən] *winken*
strain [strein] *anstrengen*
save [seiv] *außer*
strum [strʌm] *Geklimper*
interior [in'tiəriə] *Innere*
aimless ['eimlis] *ziellos*
tune [tjuːn] *Melodie*
Arab ['ærəb] *arabisch*
admit [əd'mit] *zugeben*
Eastern ['iːstən] *orientalisch*
nod [nɔd] *nicken*
ashore [ə'ʃɔː] *an Land*
study ['stʌdi] *untersuchen*
apart from [ə'pɑːt] *abgesehen von*
Diana Rea [dai'ænə 'rei]
lightless ['laitlis] *ohne Licht, dunkel*
complete [kəm'pliːt] *vollständig*
deserted [di'zəːtid] *verlassen*
all the same *trotzdem*
o' [ə] = of
junk-ship ['dʒʌŋkʃip] *Schiff zum Verschrotten*
blankness ['blæŋknis] *Verblüffung*

know—Mr. Phillepi, the foreign gentleman who's buying up a lot o' these old steamers an' taking them East to be broken up for the steel in them. Making quite a pile at it, they do tell me. Them two in front o' her belong to him, too."

"Phillepi sounds a Greek name," I said, thinking that this killed any connection with the Japs.

"That's right," said the man. "He's what you call a Levantine."

I expected Toft to be disconcerted by that, but he merely asked: "Is there anybody aboard her now?"

"On the 'Diana Rea'? I'll say so—quite a gang," said the man. "That Mr. Phillepi uses her as a depot ship for boarding an' lodging the crews that take the ships he buys out East. She's nearly always got a dozen or so aboard."

"English?" asked Toft.

"Now you've said something," growled the man with a touch of indignation. "They're foreigners—"

"Japanese?" I cried with some excitement, seeing where Toft was leading.

"Well, now, come to think of it, some might be Japs," the man said. "They keep well inboard, port regulations, you know, but I do call to mind some slant-eyed coves."

Toft shot at me another of his quick, pleased looks. He went on with his questions about the foreigners, how they lived and so forth, and whether they got their stores from local shops, for instance.

foreign ['fɔrin] *fremd, ausländisch*
a lot of [lɔt] *eine Menge*
an' [æn] = and
break up *abbrechen, verschrotten*
a pile [pail] *„ein Haufen Geld"*
them V = these
belong to [bi'lɔŋ] *gehören (zu)*
sound [saund] *klingen (wie)*
connection [kə'nekʃən] *Verbindung*
Levantine ['levəntain] *Levantiner, Orientale*
expect [iks'pekt] *erwarten*
disconcert [diskən'sə:t] *aus der Fassung bringen*
aboard [ə'bɔ:d] *an Bord*
depot ['depou] *Lagerraum*
board [bɔ:d] *verpflegen*
lodge [lɔdʒ] *unterbringen*
crew [kru:] *Mannschaft*
dozen ['dʌzn] *Dutzend*

growl [graul] *brummen, knurren*
touch [tʌtʃ] *Anflug*
indignation [indig'neiʃən] *Unwille*
foreigner ['fɔrinə] *Ausländer*
lead [li:d] *hinführen, auf etw. hinauswollen*
keep [ki:p] *sich (auf)halten*
inboard ['inbɔ:d] *innenbords, im Schiff*
port regulation [regju'leiʃən] *Hafenvorschrift*
call to mind [maind] *sich erinnern an*
slant-eyed ['sla:ntaid] *schlitzäugig*
cove *sl.* [kouv] *Bursche, Kerl*
and so forth [fɔ:θ] *und so weiter*
store [stɔ:] *Vorrat*
local ['loukəl] *örtlich, am Ort*

"In a manner o' speaking, yes," said the man. "All except the luxuries, so to speak."

"How do you mean—luxuries?"

"Well, what they call luxuries," grinned the boatman. "You wouldn't —make you sick. But foreigners like rummy grub, an' as our shops can't supply it, Mr. Phillepi sends down a car load o' the dainties they fancy every now and then. You never saw the like: mouldy cabbage, pickled cucumbers, great thick sausages—"

"And eggs?" Toft put in softly.

"You know about them eggs, hey?" the man guffawed. "Ain't they the limit? Some must have been broken in a basket I took across to the 'Diana Rea' the other day, and the niff . . .!"

"Was that yesterday morning?" Toft asked swiftly.

"Eleven o'clock night before," the man said. "They were held up by a busted tire an' kept me out of bed. But what beats me is what they want bad eggs for . . ."

It beat me, too. I was all agog by now. But when I demanded explanations fromToft, he would only mutter: "Wait until we see that rude chap at the hotel."

He was not to be seen that night, though we learnt from the waiter that his name was Scaliger. Next morning Toft went straight up to him and said with a frank smile: "This mares' nest you're hunting, Mr. Scaliger—have you made any fresh progress?"

except [ik'sept] *außer*
luxury ['lʌkʃəri] *Luxusartikel, Genußmittel*
grin [grin] *grinsen*
rummy *sl.* ['rʌmi] *„komisch"*
grub *sl.* [grʌb] *„Futter"*
supply [sə'plai] *liefern*
load [loud] *Wagenladung*
dainty ['deinti] *Leckerbissen*
fancy ['fænsi] *gern mögen*
mouldy ['mouldi] *schimmlig*
cabbage ['kæbidʒ] *Kohl*
pickled ['pikld] *gepökelt, eingesalzen*
cucumber ['kju:kəmbə] *Gurke*
sausage ['sɔsidʒ] *Wurst*
hey? [hei] *he?*
guffaw [gʌ'fɔ:] *laut lachen*
ain't V [eint] = are not
it is the limit ['limit] *das ist die Höhe*
across [ə'krɔs] *hinüber*
niff *sl.* [nif] *Gestank, Mief*
swift [swift] *schnell*
bust *sl.* [bʌst] *platzen*
that beats me F [bi:ts] *das kapiere ich nicht*
agog [ə'gɔg] *gespannt*
demand [di'ma:nd] *fragen nach*
explanation [eksplə'neiʃən] *Erklärung*
mutter ['mʌtə] *murmeln*
rude [ru:d] *grob, ungehobelt*
learnt [lə:nt] *erfuhren*
Scaliger ['skælidʒə] *Familienname*
straight up [streit] *geradewegs*
frank [fræŋk] *frei(mütig)*
progress ['prougres] *Fortschritt*

"What the devil's that to do with you?" the man growled.

"If it's anything to do with Chinese hidden in this port–I've found them," Toft sighed.

"Chinese?" Scaliger· was transformed at once. "You've found Chinese? How? Where?"

Paul Toft merely blinked at him: "Also why, Mr. Scaliger," he murmured, "why should I tell you–until I know your authority?"

"I've all the authority you need," the man snapped. "I represent the League of Nations."

"I don't think it's arms", Toft said mildly. "I feel–drugs. You're an agent of the International Drugs Commission of Geneva, aren't you?"

"How did you find that out?" he gulped.

"Oh–I didn't," Toft murmured. But he had summed up Scaliger's position so accurately that the chap caved in at once. He was, in fact, even painfully eager for Toft's help, for he was finding his task rather beyond him.

The situation was this. Drugs were being imported in wholesale but secret fashion into Great Britain. The British police had been unable to check or trace the supply, and had applied to Geneva, there the International Commission had worldwide facilities, and experience in tracking the malefactors. Geneva had come to the conclusion that Japanese smugglers were behind the business and that, in some way, the regular sailings of Japanese ships to

devil ['devl] *Teufel*
Chinese *auch Pl.* ['tʃai'ni:z] *Chinese(n)*
hidden ['hidn] *verborgen*
sigh [sai] *seufzen*
transform [træns'fɔ:m] *umwandeln*
blink [bliŋk] *zwinkern*
authority [ɔ:'θɔriti] *Befugnis*
need [ni:d] *brauchen*
snap [snæp] *hervorstoßen*
represent [repri'zent] *repräsentieren, vertreten*
League of Nations *Pl.* ['li:g əv 'neiʃənz] *Völkerbund*
arms *Pl.* [a:mz] *Waffen*
drug [drʌg] *Rauschgift*
agent ['eidʒənt] *Bevollmächtigter*
commission [kə'miʃən] *Kommission, Ausschuß*
Geneva [dʒi'ni:və] *Genf*
gulp [gʌlp] *schlucken*
sum up [sʌm] *zusammenfassen*
position [pə'ziʃən] *Stellung*
cave in F [keiv] *klein beigeben*
painfully eager for ['peinfuli 'i:gə] *heftig bemüht um*
beyond s. b. [bi'jɔnd] *über j-s Kraft*
wholesale ['houlseil] *im großen, en gros*
fashion ['fæʃən] *Weise*
check [tʃek] *eindämmen, sperren*
trace [treis] *aufspüren*
supply [sə'plai] *Zufuhr*
apply to [ə'plai] *sich wenden an*
facility [fə'siliti] *Möglichkeit, Einrichtung*
experience [iks'piəriəns] *Erfahrung*
track [træk] *aufspüren*
malefactor ['mælifæktə] *Missetäter*
conclusion [kən'klu:ʒən] *Schluß(folgerung)*

the Cornish clay ports were mixed up in it. That was the reason for Scaliger's presence in St. Frail, the most likely of the ports.

Scaliger's mother had been the daughter of a Chinese mandarin and his father an American. That explained much of his rudeness. Because he spoke Japanese and many Eastern dialects, he was naturally well qualified to tackle the Japanese. He and the Customs searched every ship entering the port, particularly the Japanese.

"Does that include vessels engaged in the coastal trade?" Toft asked. "I understand that ships trading only between English ports get a certificate that frees them from examination."

"Yes, that's so," Scaliger admitted. "We've been on the look-out for it. I can't recollect any such British coaster lying close to other ships–"

"But there is the 'Diana Rea' lying abreast the quay."

Scaliger sprang from his chair: "What do you mean–she's a mere empty hulk, like the others?"

"Not so empty," Toft said softly. "I told you there are Chinese hidden on the 'Diana Rea'."

"You're sure?" Scaliger was shaken. Then Toft told him how they had found the eggs and heard the music in the 'Diana Rea', and what the boatman had told them about her.

"Only, she belongs to Phillepi, the Greek junk merchant. He's well known–the last man I'd dream of being in such a business."

mix up [miks] *zusammenhängen*
reason ['ri:zn] *Grund*
likely ['laikli] *in Frage kommend*
mandarin ['mændərin] *Mandarin*
rudeness ['ru:dnis] *Heftigkeit*
qualified ['kwɔlifaid] *befähigt*
tackle ['tækl] *fertig werden mit*
customs *Pl.* ['kʌstəmz] *Zoll*
particularly [pə'tikjuləli] *besonders*
include [in'klu:d] *einbeziehen*
engage [in'geidʒ] *verwenden*
coastal ['koustl] *Küsten...*
trade [treid] *Schiffahrt; verkehren*
certificate [sə:'tifikit] *Bescheinigung*
free [fri:] *befreien*
examination [igzæmi'neiʃən] *Untersuchung*
be on the look-out [luk'aut] *Ausschau halten*
recollect [rekə'lekt] *sich erinnern*
coaster ['koustə] *Küstenfahrer*
mere [miə] *bloß*
empty ['empti] *leer*
hulk [hʌlk] *abgetakeltes Schiff*
hidden ['hidn] *verborgen*
shaken ['ʃeikən] *erschüttert*
junk [dʒʌŋk] *Schrott*
merchant ['mə:tʃənt] *Großhändler*

"All the better cover for the Japs. They knew you'd never suspect his ships, and they could work under your very noses. She is in an excellent position to be used by the smugglers, too. See, the quay isn't more than sixty feet from her side. The Jap comes up-stream at night, stops almost alongside her to be warped against the quay. You and the Customs can't see the dark side of her that is now so close to the 'Diana Rea'. You can't see the 'Diana Rea', either, because the Jap steamer blots her out. What's to prevent half a dozen of Japs tossing packages on to the 'Diana Rea'—the distance wouldn't be more than twenty feet?"

"By heavens, you've hit it!" cried Scaliger. "And then the dope can remain hidden on that unsuspected hulk until it's safe to trans-ship it."

"Do you know of any unexamined coastal vessel due about now?"

"The 'Spoonbill'!" Scaliger almost exploded. "She's a filthy little tramp that carries china-clay to the Lancashire canals."

In the afternoon the 'Spoonbill' came in and took up the Jap's position at the loading quays.

That night a very ordinary tug passed close to the 'Diana Rea', steaming slowly on her lawful occasions up the harbour. As she entered the shadows under the hull of the laid-up ship, a row-boat that had been concealed by the shadow of the tug cast off. Toft, Scaliger, I and three policemen were in that row-boat. In a second we were well under

cover ['kʌvə] *Schutz*
suspect [səs'pekt] *im Verdacht haben*
under your very nose *unmittelbar vor Ihrer Nase*
excellent ['eksələnt] *ausgezeichnet*
up-stream ['ʌp'striːm] *stromaufwärts*
warp [wɔːp] *bugsieren, verholen*
blot out [blɔt] *verdecken*
prevent [pri'vent] *verhindern*
toss [tɔs] *werfen*
package ['pækidʒ] *Paket*
distance ['distəns] *Entfernung*
by heavens ['hevnz] *beim Himmel*
hit [hit] *getroffen*
dope *sl.* [doup] *Rauschgift*
unsuspected ['ʌnsəs'pektid] *unverdächtig*
trans-ship [træns'ʃip] *umladen*
unexamined ['ʌnig'sæmind] *nicht kontrolliert*
due [djuː] *fällig*
spoon-bill ['spuːnbil] *Löffelreiher (hier Schiffsname)*
filthy ['filθi] *schmutzig*
tramp [træmp] *Trampschiff*
Lancashire ['læŋkəʃiə] *englische Grafschaft*
canal [kə'næl] *(Schiffahrts)Kanal*
loading ['loudiŋ] *Lade...*
tug [tʌg] *Schlepper*
lawful ['lɔːful] *rechtmäßig*
occasion [ə'keiʒən] *Anlaß, Gelegenheit*
hull [hʌl] *(Schiffs)Rumpf*
row-boat ['roubout] *Ruderboot*
conceal [kən'siːl] *verbergen*
cast off [kaːst] *stieß ab*

the overhang of the 'Diana Rea's' stern. The 'Spoonbill' lay against the quay some sixty feet away. The world became dark, noiseless.

But just before midnight something did happen.

Quite abruptly there was a soft swish from the blackness above us, then a sound like the softest of blows from the 'Spoonbill'. Minutes passed, nothing happened. Toft caught my arm, whispered: "In the air–well forward," and there, a degree blacker than the night, I saw a big, case-like shape moving from the shadow of the 'Diana Rea'– floating through the air.

We sat spellbound. The case went gliding through the air, noiselessly, and making for the 'Spoonbill'. Toft acted. Getting his hands against the plates of the 'Diana Rea', he drew our boat forward. Just above our heads was the blackness of a cargo door low in her. From it we saw a spider thread of rope stretching over our heads towards the 'Spoonbill'.

Scaliger half rose to climb in through the door. Toft checked him until the rope slacked and sagged. A soft voice above us spoke an order. The hauling gear stopped. Toft flashed a signal shorewards with his electric torch.

As his spider-long arms reached up to the sill of the cargo door and heaved his lank body inside, an uproar broke out on the 'Spoonbill', as police concealed about the quay boarded her. But we had no minds

overhang ['ouvəhæŋ] *Überhang, Vorsprung*
stern [stə:n] *Heck*
noiseless ['nɔizlis] *laut-, geräuschlos*
abrupt [ə'brʌpt] *plötzlich*
soft [sɔft] *leise, leicht*
swish [swiʃ] *Rascheln, Schwirren, Sausen*
blow [blou] *Schlag, Stoß*
whisper ['wispə] *flüstern*
well forward ['fɔ:wəd] *genau vorn, gerade vor uns*
degree [di'gri:] *Grad*
case-like ['keislaik] *kistenähnlich*
shape [ʃeip] *Gestalt, Form*
float [flout] *schweben*
spellbound ['spelbaund] *(wie) gebannt*
glide [glaid] *gleiten*
make for *sich zubewegen auf*
act [ækt] *handeln*
drew [dru:] *zog*
cargo door ['ka:gou] *Lade-, Frachtluke*
low [lou] *niedrig*
spider thread ['spaidə-'θred] *Spinnenfaden*
rope [roup] *Seil*
stretch [stretʃ] *sich spannen*
rose [rouz] *erhob sich*
climb [klaim] *klettern*
check [tʃek] *zurückhalten*
slack [slæk] *schlaff werden*
sag [sæg] *durchhängen*
hauling gear ['hɔ:liŋ giə] *Fördergetriebe*
flash [flæʃ] *aufblitzen lassen*
shorewards ['ʃɔ:wədz] *landwärts*
electric torch [i'lektrik 'tɔ:tʃ] *Taschenlampe*
sill [sil] *Schwelle*
heave [hi:v] *hochziehen, hieven*
lank [læŋk] *schlank*
uproar ['ʌprɔ:] *Aufruhr*
board [bɔ:d] *an Bord gehen*

for that. We could hear Toft fighting for his life on the 'Diana Rea'.

mind [maind] *Sinn*

There were Chinese smugglers aboard her, half a dozen, plus other scourings of the seas. And they fought like cornered rats. Things might have gone ill with us had not a boat-load of police, putting off at Toft's signal, arrived to win the day. The 'Spoonbill' was short-handed, also they were taken by surprise—fortunately; else they would have flung the case we had seen into the harbour and we might have lost direct evidence.

It was a big, stout packing-case, bound with iron bands, and it was full of lumps of china-clay. When they were broken open, packages of deadly drugs were found. On the 'Diana Rea' we found more china-clay, also evidence that lumps had been reduced to powder and then moulded round the drug parcels again into fresh lumps. There was also evidence that the Japs had brought the drugs in a watertight cask, which they had thrown overboard at the end of a buoyed line for the Chinese on the 'Diana Rea' to recover.

scourings *Pl.* ['skauriŋz] *Abschaum*
corner ['kɔːnə] *in die Enge treiben*
rat [ræt] *Ratte*
ill [il] *böse, schlimm*
boat-load ['boutloud] *Bootsbesatzung*
put off *abstoßen*
win the day [win] *Sieger bleiben*
be short-handed ['ʃɔːt-'hændid] *zu wenige Mann Besatzung haben*
be taken by surprise [sə'praiz] *völlig überrascht sein*
fortunately ['fɔːtʃnitli] *zum Glück*
flung [flʌŋ] *geworfen*
evidence ['evidəns] *Beweis(stück)*
stout [staut] *stark, fest*
bound [baund] *hier: beschlagen*
iron band ['aiən'bænd] *Eisenband*
lump [lʌmp] *Klumpen, Stück*
deadly ['dedli] *tödlich, giftig*
reduce [ri'djuːs] *zerkleinern, verwandeln*
powder ['paudə] *Pulver, Staub*
mould [mould] *formen*
watertight ['wɔːtətait] *wasserdicht*
cask [kɑːsk] *Faß*
throw overboard ['ouvəbɔːd] *über Bord werfen*
buoyed line [bɔid] *Schwimmleine*
recover [ri'kʌvə] *einholen, auffischen*
hawser ['hɔːsə] *Trosse*
aerial transporter ['ɛəriəl] *Transportvorrichtung in der Luft*

The rest of the process was easy. A light line was flung to the 'Spoonbill', and this drawing a stronger hawser between the two ships, a perfect aerial transporter made trans-shipment easy under cover of the darkness. When the cases full of doped lumps reached the 'Spoonbill' they were emptied on top of the ordinary cargo of china-clay lumps.

empty ['empti] *(aus)leeren*

Three cases of such faked lumps had been prepared for trans-shipment on this occasion. They contained enough drugs to poison a city. And yet the extraordinary cleverness of the thing had made the ghastly traffic almost foolproof.

"And they would have gone on getting away with it as they have for months", Scaliger said after he had made his arrests, including that of Phillepi, "and I'd still be hunting that mare's nest but for you, Mr. Toft."

"And those bad eggs?" I chuckled.

"And his knowledge that since only Chinese ate bad eggs, he must look for them as the core of the mystery," Scaliger said.

But Paul Toft had the last word.

"Oh, no," he smiled. "You must remember, Doctor, I felt something wrong even before we found the eggs. And even the eggs themselves —I felt their badness was from something more than smell."

(From: Pearson's Magazine. London.)

fake F [feik] *nachmachen*
prepare [pri'pɛə] *vorbereiten*
contain [kən'tein] *enthalten*
poison ['pɔizn] *vergiften*
extraordinary [iks'trɔːdnri] *außerordentlich*
cleverness ['klevənis] *Klugheit*
ghastly ['gɑːstli] *gespenstisch*
foolproof ['fuːlpruːf] *narrensicher*
arrest [ə'rest] *Verhaftung*
including [in'kluːdiŋ] *einschließlich*
but for you *wenn Sie nicht gewesen wären*
chuckle ['tʃʌkl] *kichern*
knowledge ['nɔlidʒ] *Kenntnis*
since [sins] *da*
core [kɔː] *Kern*
smell [smel] *Geruch*

Death, Fire, and Life

By A. Bennett

I.

Mr. Curtenty lay in bed in the winter morning darkness, and reflected upon the horrible injustice of destiny. Mr. Curtenty was a most respectable gentleman. He had never done anything wrong; his conscience was sinless. In sixty years his dignity and his respectability had not been ever compromised. He could, and he did, look everybody unyieldingly in the face. By nature and long practice he was intensely proud and independent. All the world addressed him as "Mr.". Once he had lost a situation through his employer omitting the "Mr.". Of course he had not openly resented the omission, for he was not a fool, but the omission had put him in a frame of mind favourable to quarrelling, and a quarrel about some trifle had ensued. Nevertheless he had soon obtained a new situation, which unhappily he had lost through the death of the new employer.

Since that disaster—now rather more than a year ago—he had been workless, and therefore wageless. Society seemed to blame him for being sixty years old. The fact that he had no particular trade also counted against him. He had always had posts such as watchman, door-keeper, timekeeper, inspector—posts which meant doing nothing with dignity.

reflect [ri'flekt] *nachdenken*
destiny ['destini] *Schicksal*
conscience ['kɔnʃəns] *Gewissen*
sinless ['sinlis] *unschuldig, rein*
dignity ['digniti] *Würde*
respectability [rispektə'biliti] *Ansehen*
compromise ['kɔmprəmaiz] *gefährden*
unyielding [ʌn'jiːldiŋ] *unbeugsam*
practice ['præktis] *Übung, Gewohnheit*
independent [indi'pendənt] *unabhängig*
employer [im'plɔiə] *Arbeitgeber, Chef*
omit [ou'mit] *weglassen*
resent [ri'zent] *übelnehmen*
frame of mind ['freim əv 'maind] *(Gemüts)Verfassung*
favourable ['feivərəbl] *günstig, geneigt*
trifle ['traifl] *Kleinigkeit*
ensue [in'sjuː] *darauf folgen*
nevertheless [nevəðə'les] *dennoch*
obtain [əb'tein] *erhalten*
rather [rɑːðə] *eher, noch*
wageless ['weidʒlis] *ohne Verdienst*
society [sə'saiəti] *Gesellschaft*
blame [bleim] *zum Vorwurf machen*
particular [pə'tikjulə] *besonders*
count [kaunt] *zählen*
watchman ['wɔtʃmən] *(Nacht)Wächter*
timekeeper ['taimkiːpə] *(Arbeitszeit)Kontrolleur*

Hence no doubt his feeling of superiority to people who actually did things.

Somehow he could scarcely hide this feeling—even from his daughter's husband, who secretly resented it. Jim Crowther was a young miner living at Longshaw, and in the opinion of Mr. Curtenty, Jim's wife, Harriet, had married beneath her. Every week he disliked Jim and Harriet more and more, because they were contributing to his subsistence. They were not so crude in their methods of charity as to give him money direct. Certainly not. Such clumsiness would have made an everlasting breach between the two generations. Mr. Curtenty knew naught, officially, of any help. Only it invariably happened that when Curtenty had not a shilling, Mrs. Curtenty had ten shillings or so, which she produced as it were apologetically. Mr. Curtenty was diplomatic enough never to inquire whence she had obtained the money.

Thus the twelve lean months had run precariously and unsatisfactorily on.

But a crisis was now upon Mr. Curtenty. For his wife had told him that Harriet had told her that Jim had told Harriet that Mrs. Curtenty could go and live with the Crowthers at Longshaw if she liked, and Mr. Curtenty too. And little by little Mr. Curtenty was given to understand that either he must submit to this humiliation—or starve. Well, Mr. Curtenty had his pride, and he swore to himself that he would not submit

hence [hens] *daher*
doubt [daut] *Zweifel*
superiority [sjuːpiəri'ɔriti] *Überlegenheit*
scarcely ['skɛəsli] *kaum*
miner ['mainə] *Bergmann*
Longshaw ['lɔŋʃɔː] *erfundener Ortsname*
opinion [ə'pinjən] *Meinung*
beneath her [bi'niːθ] *unter ihrem Stande*
contribute [kən'tribjuːt] *beisteuern*
subsistence [səb'sistəns] *(Lebens)Unterhalt*
crude [kruːd] *roh*
charity ['tʃæriti] *Wohltätigkeit*
clumsiness ['klʌmzinis] *Taktlosigkeit*
everlasting [evə'lɑːstiŋ] *dauernd*
breach [briːtʃ] *Bruch*
naught [nɔːt] *nichts*
invariable [in'vɛəriəbl] *gleichbleibend*
produce [prə'djuːs] *hervorholen*
as it were *sozusagen*
apologetical [əpɔlə'dʒetikəl] *entschuldigend*
inquire [in'kwaiə] *sich erkundigen*
whence [wens] *woher*

lean [liːn] *mager*
precarious [pri'kɛəriəs] *unsicher*
unsatisfactory ['ʌnsætis'fæktəri] *unbefriedigend*
crisis ['kraisis] *Wendepunkt*
live with [liv] *wohnen bei*
little by little *nach und nach*
submit [səb'mit] *unterwerfen*
humiliation [hjuːmili'eiʃən] *Demütigung*
starve [stɑːv] *verhungern*
pride [praid] *Stolz*
swore [swɔː] *schwor*

to it. He simply could not imagine himself as a helpless pauper dependent in the home of his son-in-law. He conveyed his decision to Mrs. Curtenty, and the next thing he heard was that if he wouldn't go she would! Ah! He saw well enough that the notion was to force him into submission! As if anybody could force him into submission!

Two days previously, it being a Wednesday, Mr. Curtenty had been informed that Mrs. Curtenty would migrate to Longshaw at the end of the week, Saturday. It was now Friday. The supreme catastrophe was indeed shaping.

His ear caught a puffpuff—puffpuff, the same being the first irregular coughings of the engine of Clayhanger's Steam Printing Works. These coughings were Mr. Curtenty's morning clock—he had no other, nor watch either. The hour was seven. Mr. Curtenty slid out of bed, and began with deliberation to dress. The first part of his dressing he did in the dark. Then he lit a candle, behind the bed's head, and with a morsel of blacking and an old stumpy brush he softly cleaned his boots—or such poor fragments of them as were left to clean.

A miserable small room, but the totality of Mr. Curtenty's home! Once he had rented a whole house, and could walk from one room to another and go upstairs and downstairs and still be at home ... A few pitiable bits of furniture, including the little oil-stove on which his wife cooked

imagine [i'mædʒin] *vorstellen*
pauper ['pɔːpə] *Almosenempfänger*
dependent [di'pendənt] *abhängig*
son-in-law ['sʌninlɔː] *Schwiegersohn*
convey [kən'vei] *mitteilen*
decision [di'siʒən] *Entscheidung*
notion ['nouʃən] *Absicht*
force [fɔːs] *zwingen*
submission [səb'miʃən] *Unterwerfung*
previously ['priːvjəsli] *vorher*
migrate [mai'greit] *fortziehen*
supreme [sjuː'priːm] *höchst, äußerst*
shape [ʃeip] *Gestalt annehmen*
caught [kɔːt] *nahm auf*
irregular [i'regjulə] *unregelmäßig*
cough [kɔf] *Keuchen*
engine ['endʒin] *Maschine*
print [print] *drucken*
watch [wɔtʃ] *Taschenuhr*
slid [slid] *glitt*
deliberation [dilibə'reiʃən] *Überlegung*
lit [lit] *zündete an*
candle ['kændl] *Kerze*
head [hed] *Kopfende*
morsel ['mɔːsəl] *Stückchen*
blacking ['blækiŋ] *Schuhkrem*
stumpy ['stʌmpi] *hier: abgenutzt*
soft [sɔft] *sacht*
fragment ['frægmənt] *Überrest*
miserable ['mizərəbl] *armselig*
totality [tou'tæliti] *Gesamtheit, Ganze*
rent [rent] *mieten*
pitiable ['pitiəbl] *erbärmlich*
furniture ['fəːnitʃə] *Möbel*
oil-stove ['ɔilstouv] *Petroleumofen*

their so-called meals! Once she had held sway over a whole kitchen-range!

On the old tin tray was just enough bread, and dripping, and bits of cured fish to last them till the next morning. Thenceforward, the fiat had been issued from Longshaw, there were to be no more supplies. And then what? He knew that his wife was wondering, and Harriet was wondering, and Jim was wondering what the obstinate, secretive old man would do–what would happen. He alone knew what would happen.

When he had laced his boots under the candle, and combed his hair, he extinguished the candle and finished his toilet in the dark. But the dark was now twilight; the earth was revolving as usual, and in its revolution baring Bursley to the dawn. Mr. Curtenty buttoned his greenish jacket, tied an antique woollen muffler round his collarless neck, put on his cap, and went forth into Woodisun Lane.

He knew he would be too early. He always was too early. He paced smartly but with dignity about Duck Square. A huge tram, packed with people who had work and were going off to it, rumbled past. Mr. Curtenty stamped his feet into the pavement and rubbed his hands, for January mornings are always dank and chill in the Five Towns. Yet while doing this he pretended with diginity not to feel the cold. At last he descried the postman, and returned to the front door of the cottage in which

hold sway over [swei] *herrschen über*
kitchen range ['kitʃin-'reindʒ] *Kochherd*
tin [tin] *Zinn, Blech*
tray [trei] *Tablett*
dripping ['dripiŋ] *Bratenfett*
cure [kjuə] *räuchern*
last [lɑːst] *reichen für*
thence forward ['ðens-'fɔːwəd] *von da an*
fiat ['faiæt] *Machtspruch, Befehl*
issue ['isjuː] *ausgeben*
supplies *Pl.* [sə'plaiz] *Versorgung, Proviant*
wonder ['wʌndə] *sich fragen*
obstinate ['ɔbstinit] *halsstarrig*
secretive [si'kriːtiv] *verschlossen*
lace [leis] *zuschnüren*
comb [koum] *kämmen*
extinguish [iks'tiŋgwiʃ] *(aus)löschen*
twilight ['twailait] *Zwielicht*
revolve [ri'vɔlv] *sich drehen*
revolution [revə'luːʃən] *Umdrehung*
bare [bɛə] *bloßlegen*
dawn [dɔːn] *Dämmerung*
button ['bʌtn] *zuknöpfen*
greenish ['griːniʃ] *grünlich*
tie [tai] *binden*
antique [æn'tiːk] *altmodisch*
muffler ['mʌflə] *Schal*
collarless ['kɔləlis] *kragenlos*
pace [peis] *schreiben, gehen*
smart [smɑːt] *flink*
packed [pækt] *zum Bersten voll*
rumble past ['rʌmbl 'pɑːst] *vorbeirasseln, -rumpeln*
pavement ['peivmənt] *Bürgersteig*
rub [rʌb] *reiben*
dank [dæŋk] *naßkalt*
chill [tʃil] *frostig*
Five Towns *heute: Stoke-on-Trent*

he occupied one room; and he received the postman majestically on the doorstep.

"Good morning," said the genial postman.

"Good morning to you," said Mr. Curtenty grandly, and took from the postman a small yellow official envelope. In the privacy of the cottage stairs he opened the envelope. Its contents were quite in order: an authority to withdraw the sum of two shillings from the Savings-Bank department of the Post Office. Then Mr. Curtenty drew from his breast-pocket a yellowish bank-book, which showed that twenty pounds stood to his credit, and he carefully put the withdrawal form within the book and replaced the book in his pocket.

Surely you are not surprised! A prudent man must have something up his sleeve for the last emergencies. Mr. Curtenty had maintained that twenty pounds in reserve throughout a year of privation and humiliation. He had lied about it for a year and more than a year. No matter how terrible a plight you may be in, it is always possible to conceive yourself in a still worse plight. That twenty pounds was Mr. Curtenty's bulwark against the imaginable worse—the fear of which had plagued him for forty years. It was the last defence and resource of his independence.

"Where ye been?" asked his waking wife, as he re-entered their home.

"Getting a breath of air," said Mr. Curtenty.

pretend [pri'tend] *so tun als ob*
descry [dis'krai] *entdekken*
cottage ['kɔtidʒ] *kleines Wohnhaus*

---

occupy ['ɔkjupai] *bewohnen*
genial ['dʒiːnjəl] *freundlich*
grand [grænd] *vornehm, würdevoll*
envelope ['enviloup] *Umschlag*
privacy ['praivəsi] *Ruhe, Zurückgezogenheit*
authority [ɔː'θɔriti] *Vollmacht, Anweisung*
withdraw [wið'drɔː] *abheben*
savings-bank ['seiviŋz-bæŋk] *Sparkasse*
credit ['kredit] *Guthaben*
withdrawal form [wið-'drɔːəl] *Abhebungsformular*
replace [ri'pleis] *zurückstecken*
surprise [sə'praiz] *überraschen*
prudent ['pruːdənt] *umsichtig*
have s. th. up one's sleeve [sliːv] *etw. in Reserve haben*
emergency [i'məːdʒənsi] *Not(lage)*
maintain [men'tein] *(be)halten*
reserve [ri'zəːv] *Reserve*
throughout [θruː'aut] *während, hindurch*
privation [prai'veiʃən] *Entbehrung*
no matter ['mætə] *es hat nichts zu sagen*
terrible ['terəbl] *schrecklich*
plight [plait] *Notlage*
conceive [kən'siːv] *vorstellen*
bulwark ['bulwək] *Bollwerk*
imaginable [i'mædʒinəbl] *denkbar*
plague [pleig] *plagen*
resource [ri'sɔːs] *Zuflucht*

II.

In the evening, about half-past seven, Mrs. Curtenty was lying in bed (for warmth) and Mr. Curtenty was sitting on one of the two chairs, all in the dark, when Mr. Curtenty, after a little shuffling of his legs and scrunching of the chair legs on the bare boards, suddenly rose and felt his way to the door, where his cap and muffler hung on a hook. The pair had had two lean meals and one snack; all the fish was eaten, but not quite all the bread; some tea remained for breakfast. Mr. Curtenty had been abroad once, in the afternoon, and during that period he had cashed the warrant for two shillings. Whether or not his wife had gone out in the same interval he did not know. They had scarcely spoken to each other, not from unfriendliness, but from habit. Not a word had been said about the morrow. All she said was, as Mr. Curtenty fumbled on the cheek of the door: "Where ye going?"

And all he replied was:

"A breath of air."

He left without looking at the companion of his life. Even if he had looked at her he could not have seen her in the darkness. Still, he might have lit the last inch of candle for a few seconds and looked at her, for the moment was one of farewell after a companionship of thirty years. But his sentimental emotions had been numbed, frozen by misfortune, by spiritual pride, by privation, by secretiveness, by hidden anger against

independence [indi'pendəns] *Unabhängigkeit*
where ye? [jiː] = where have you?, where are you?
get a breath of air [breθ] *ein bißchen Luft schnappen*

---

warmth [wɔːmθ] *Wärme*
shuffle ['ʃʌfl] *schlurfen*
scrunch [skrʌntʃ] *krachen*
bare [bɛə] *bloß*
board [bɔːd] *Diele(nbrett)*
felt his way to *tastete sich zu*
hook [huk] *Haken*
lean [liːn] *mager*
snack [snæk] *Imbiß*
abroad [ə'brɔːd] *draußen*
cash [kæʃ] *einlösen*
warrant ['wɔrənt] *(Rück-) Zahlungsanweisung*
whether ['weðə] *ob*
interval ['intəvəl] *Zwischenzeit*
scarcely ['skɛəsli] *kaum*
habit ['hæbit] *Gewohnheit*
fumble ['fʌmbl] *umhertasten*
cheek [tʃiːk] *Seitenteil, Rahmen*
companion [kəm'pænjən] *Gefährtin*
lit [lit] *angezündet*
inch [intʃ] *Zoll (2,54 cm)*
farewell ['fɛə'wel] *Abschied*
companionship [kəm'pænjənʃip] *Gemeinschaft*
sentimental [senti'mentl] *gefühlvoll*
emotion [i'mouʃən] *Regung*
numb [nʌm] *betäuben, erstarren*
misfortune [mis'fɔːtʃən] *Unglück*
spiritual ['spiritjuəl] *geistig*
secretiveness [si'kriːtivnis] *Verschlossenheit*
hidden ['hidn] *verborgen*
anger ['æŋgə] *Zorn*
fate [feit] *Schicksal*

fate, and by self-righteousness. So he just went. He knew that his wife would fall asleep and stay asleep.

It was a raw night in Woodisun Lane, and a muddy.

He had not meant to visit the Free Reference Library in the Wedgwood Institution, but as a measure of precaution he decided to do so. He was at home in that warm refuge of the unemployed, the Wedgwood Institution. The horrid, stuffy, damp smell of the Reference Library delighted his nose. After the usual formalities he obtained Quain's Dictionary of Medicine, and, taking the thick volume to a desk, he turned over its pages.

His brain was absolutely clear. He was not out of his mind, nor out of any part of his mind. In no circumstances would he migrate to his son-in-law's. His wife might go; she indeed would go; and she would be happy there, or at least contented. The twenty pounds (less two shillings) which he had guarded for an ultimate contingency would be useless to him, because too soon exhausted. He might of course fend for himself, all alone, for a time on the twenty pounds; but if he did so his family would know for sure that he had had a secret hoard after all, and he could not bear that revelation; it would too seriously humiliate him. Moreover, when the twenty pounds was gone—what then? Merely the same crucial, unanswerable problem as now! No! He had had enough, and

self-righteousness ['self'raitʃəsnis] *Selbstgerechtigkeit*
fall asleep [ə'sliːp] *einschlafen*
raw [rɔː] *rauh, naßkalt*
muddy ['mʌdi] *trüb*
free reference liberary ['refrəns 'laibrəri] *öffentliche Handbibliothek*
measure ['meʒə] *Maßnahme*
precaution [pri'kɔːʃən] *Vorsichtsmaßregel*
refuge ['refjuːdʒ] *Zufluchtsort*
unemployed ['ʌnim'plɔid] *arbeitslos*
horrid ['hɔrid] *scheußlich*
stuffy ['stʌfi] *stickig*
damp [dæmp] *feucht*
smell [smel] *Geruch*
delight [di'lait] *erfreuen*
formalities *Pl.* [fɔː'mælitiz] *Formalitäten*
obtain [əb'tein] *erhalten*
volume ['vɔljum] *Band*
turn over *umblättern*
be out of one's mind [maind] *von Sinnen sein*
circumstance ['səːkəmstəns] *Umstand*
contented [kən'tentid] *zufrieden* *[ren*
guard [gɑːd] *aufbewah-*
ultimate ['ʌltimit] *letzt*
contingency [kən'tindʒənsi] *unvorhergesehener Fall*
exhaust [ig'zɔːst] *erschöpfen*
fend [fend] *sorgen*
for sure [ʃuə] *sicher*
secret ['siːkrit] *heimlich*
hoard [hɔːd] *Hort, Schatz*
revelation [revi'leiʃən] *Enthüllung*
humiliate [hjuː'milieit] *demütigen*
moreover [mɔː'rouvə] *außerdem*
merely ['miəli] *bloß, nur*
crucial ['kruːʃjəl] *schwierig*

there could be but one answer to the question: To be or not to be?

Quain was perfectly explicit: "The soluble cyanides, more especially the cyanide of potassium, largely used by photographers and by electroplaters, are common articles of commerce, and produce the same deadly results as the acid itself. The fatal dose of prussic acid is the equivalent of less than one grain of the anhydrous acid."

Nothing could be simpler to the understanding. He had read it before, but he wished to refresh his memory and so avoid the possibility of blunder. He refrained from proceeding to read about the effect of the poison; he had read that also before; it was rather disturbing, sensational.

He closed the stately tome and grandly handed it back across the counter to the pert young thing in a jersey who had dominion there. None could have guessed, as he calmly descended the broad steps of the Institution, that he was solemnly marked out and divided that night from every other soul in the town.

He made his way to Critchlow's in St. Luke's Square, the oldest chemist in Bursley. Critchlow's, however, was closed. Monstrous that the shop should be closed on that night of all nights! Holl's clock across the Square showed six minutes to eight, and Critchlow's had no right to be closed until eight. But Critchlow's was closed.

Mr. Curtenty had purposely driven the transaction as late as convenient,

explicit [iks'plisit] *deutlich*
soluble ['sɔljubl] *löslich*
cyanide of potassium ['saiənaid əv pə'tæsjəm] *Zyankali*
electroplater [i'lektroupleitə] *Galvaniseur*
commerce ['kɔməːs] *Handel*
acid ['æsid] *Säure*
fatal ['feitl] *tödlich*
dose [dous] *Dosis*
prussic acid ['prʌsik] *Blausäure*
equivalent of [i'kwivələnt] *gleiche Menge wie*
grain [grein] *Gran* (65 mg)
anhydrous [æn'haidrəs] *wasserfrei*
avoid [ə'vɔid] *vermeiden*
blunder ['blʌndə] *Fehler*
refrain [ri'frein] *es unterlassen*
proceed [prə'siːd] *fortfahren*
poison ['pɔizn] *Gift*
disturbing [dis'təːbiŋ] *beunruhigend*
stately ['steitli] *stattlich*
tome [toum] *Band, Buch*
counter ['kauntə] *(Laden)Tisch*
pert [pəːt] *schnippisch*
jersey ['dʒəːsi] *Strickjacke*
dominion [də'minjən] *(Ober)Herrschaft*
guess [ges] *vermuten*
calm [kaːm] *ruhig*
solemn ['sɔləm] *gewichtig*
mark out [maːk] *hervorheben*
chemist ['kemist] *Apotheker*
monstrous ['mɔnstrəs] *gräßlich*
that night of all nights *ausgerechnet an dem Abend*
purposely ['pəːpəsli] *absichtlich*
transaction [træn'zækʃən] *Unternehmung*
convenient [kən'viːnjənt] *passend, möglich*

for he desired a deserted, nocturnal town for his mortal work; but he now saw the possibility of having cut the thing too fine. Still, there was Salter's, in the Market Place—all on the way to the empty playground, beyond the Town Hall, which he had selected for his end. He walked to the top of the Square, and turned to the right where the Market Place was. He had an idea that Salter's kept open till nine o'clock. Salter's was open, and he entered the shop, which happened to be empty behind the counter as well as in front of it.

Salter's was the new chemistry in Bursley. A fine, young gentleman, Mr. Salter himself, appeared from the dark backward of the establishment, glided along the length of the counter, and became a note of interrogation to Mr. Curtenty, whose tongue—very surprisingly—clave to his palate and whose throat grew parched.

"I want some Scheele's Acid."

Mr. Salter stared at Mr. Curtenty, and Mr. Curtenty, invigorated and challenged by the stare, returned it.

"Photographic work?"

Mr. Curtenty nodded. "Aye!"

"How much?"

"Dun' know. Smallish bottle."

"Half a pint?"

"Aye! That'll do."

"I'll get you to sign the poison book."

"Aye!"

Mr. Salter moved about behind the counter, and in a startlingly brief

desire [di'zaiə] *wünschen*
deserted [di'zə:tid] *menschenleer*
nocturnal [nɔk'tə:nl] *nächtlich*
mortal ['mɔ:tl] *todbringend*
cut s. th. too fine *sl. etw. zu knapp berechnen*
empty ['empti] *leer*
playground ['pleigraund] *Spielplatz*
beyond [bi'jɔnd] *jenseits*
town hall ['taun 'hɔ:l] *Rathaus*
select [si'lekt] *auswählen*
top [tɔp] *oberes Ende*
idea [ai'diə] *Ahnung*
kept open *war geöffnet*
happen to be . . . *zufällig . . . sein*
chemistry ['kemistri] *Apotheke*
backward ['bækwəd] *Hintergrund*
establishment [is'tæbliʃmənt] *Geschäft*
length [leŋθ] *Länge, Längsseite*
note of interrogation [interə'geiʃən] *Fragezeichen*
tongue [tʌŋ] *Zunge*
clave [kleiv] *(veraltet) klebte*
palate ['pælit] *Gaumen*
throat [θrout] *Kehle*
parch [pa:tʃ] *ausdörren*
Scheele's acid *Blausäure (nach schwed. Chemiker)*
stare [stɛə] *starren; Starren*
invigorate [in'vigəreit] *stärken, kräftigen*
challenge ['tʃælindʒ] *herausfordern*
aye [ai] *ja*
dun' V [dʌn] = don't
pint [paint] *Pinte (0,57 l)*
sign [sain] *unterschreiben*

startling ['sta:tliŋ] *überraschend*
brief [bri:f] *kurz*

space of time was slapping a salmon-tinted poison label on a corked bottle. The next instant he had screwed the bottle into a bit of wrapping-paper, and he was in the act of handing it to Mr. Curtenty when a great lady entered the shop and Mr. Salter turned to her with eager and yet dignified deference, excusing himself negligently to Mr. Curtenty.

But Mr. Curtenty held the bottle. He held it victoriously; and it was no longer a bottle in a bit of paper—it was a sacred phial, magic, omnipotent, more powerful than man and than God.

"One-and-twopence, please," murmured Mr. Salter, between two respectful sentences addressed to the lady.

"One-and-twopence!" cried Mr. Curtenty, dropping the florin, which he was holding suspended in mid pocket. "One-and-twopence! Why! It hadn't ought to be more than tenpence-half-penny!"

"I'm afraid it's one-and-two," said Mr. Salter, calmly.

"Not me!" Mr. Curtenty growled with finality, and, dropping the bottle on to the round india-rubber mat intended to receive coins, he walked with fury and grandeur out of the shop, not caring for forty Salters nor forty great ladies.

People passing in the Market Place heard and saw Mr. Curtenty muttering and chuntering to himself. He noticed with resentment that he was observed, and walked off in the direction of Hanbridge. His resolution

space [speis] *Raum*
slap [slæp] *klatschen*
salmon-tinted ['sæmən-'tintid] *lachsfarben*
label ['leibl] *Etikett*
cork [kɔːk] *verkorken*
instant ['instənt] *Augenblick*
screw [skruː] *hier: einwickeln*
wrapping-paper ['ræpiŋ] *Einwickelpapier*
eager ['iːgə] *eifrig*
dignified ['dignifaid] *würdevoll*
deference ['defərəns] *Ehrerbietung*
negligent ['neglidʒənt] *nachlässig*
victorious [vik'tɔːriəs] *siegreich*
sacred ['seikrid] *geweiht, heilig*
phial ['faiəl] *Fläschchen*
magic ['mædʒik] *voll magischer Kraft*
omnipotent [ɔm'nipətənt] *allmächtig*
one-and-twopence ['tʌpəns] *1 Shilling, 2 Pence*
murmur ['məːmə] *murmeln*
florin ['flɔrin] *Zweischillingstück*
suspended [səs'pendid] *in der Schwebe*
in mid pocket *im mittleren Teil der Tasche*
why! *nanu!*
halfpenny ['heipni] *halber Penny*
I'm afraid [ə'freid] *leider*
growl [graul] *knurren, brummen*
finality [fai'næliti] *Entschiedenheit*
india-rubber ['indjə-'rʌbə] *Gummi*
mat [mæt] *Matte*
fury ['fjuəri] *Zorn*
grandeur ['grændʒə] *Würde*
mutter ['mʌtə] *murmeln*
chunter ['tʃʌntə] *vor sich hinmurmeln*

to carry out his plan was as firm as ever—for nothing could shake it—but he was equally determined not to be done in the eye.

III.

Woodisun Lane is one of the ways from Bursley to Hanbridge. Indeed, from Bursley Market Place it is the shortest and the oldest way, but by far the worst way, by reason of its gradients and its foul surface. However, Mr. Curtenty took it, in order, by a glance at the window of his home, to see whether Mrs. Curtenty was wastefully burning the last inch of the candle. She was not; the window gave no sign of light. Strange to say, Mrs. Curtenty's thriftiness disappointed him, because he wanted another grievance, he wanted dozens of grievances, to gather into his breast as St. Sebastian gathered arrows.

He had to be content with the one great grievance against Mr. Salter—Mr. Salter, who by his rapacity was forcing a determined and desperate man to walk unnecessarily over to Hanbridge on a dank night.

Nearly at the top of the hill, at Bleakridge, Woodisun Lane debouches into the main thoroughfare, Trafalgar Road. Somewhat farther on is the football ground, and then there is a corner upon which had stood for centuries a small earthenware manufactory—one small manufactory succeeding another there from Plantagenet times onwards. Young Eddie Colclough had recently

resentment [ri'zentmənt] *Groll*
resolution [rezə'lu:ʃən] *Entschluß*

---

carry out *ausführen*
equally ['i:kwəli] *ebenso*
determined [di'tə:mind] *entschlossen*
do s. b. in the eye F *j-n „übers Ohr hauen"*

by reason ['ri:zn] *wegen*
gradient ['greidjənt] *Steigung*
foul [faul] *schmutzig*
surface ['sə:fis] *Straßendecke*
glance [glɑ:ns] *flüchtiger Blick*
wasteful ['weistful] *verschwenderisch*
strange to say [streindʒ] *seltsamerweise*
thriftiness ['θriftinis] *Sparsamkeit*
disappoint [disə'pɔint] *enttäuschen*
grievance ['gri:vəns] *Grund zur Klage*
St. Sebastian [snt si'bæstjən] *St. Sebastian*
arrow ['ærou] *Pfeil*
content [kən'tent] *zufrieden*
rapacity [rə'pæsiti] *Habgier*
desperate ['despərit] *verzweifelt*
unnecessary [ʌn'nesisəri] *unnötig*
debouch [di'bautʃ] *einmünden*
main thoroughfare ['mein 'θʌrəfɛə] *Hauptverkehrsstraße*
earthenware ['ə:θənwɛə] *Steingut*
manufactory [mænju'fæktəri] *(veraltet) Fabrik*
succeed [sək'si:d] *(nach-) folgen*
Plantagenet [plæn'tædʒənet] *(Beiname des engl. Königshauses von 1154 bis 1485)*

razed a small manufactory to the ground and was just finishing the erection of a new one of an experimental type wherein various modern dodges of economic organization were to be tested.

As he passed the building Mr. Curtenty's watchman's nose sniffed the air, in the manner of a tiger sniffing distant blood. Mr. Curtenty became a nose and nothing but a nose; and his grievance and his purpose were equally forgotten. It might be said that Mr. Curtenty had no trade, but that he had a profession was richly demonstrated in that sniffing moment. He sniffed the night-watchman's arch-foe – smoke, indicating fire.

He looked at the façade, whose upper windows were still unglazed, and could see no curling wisp of smoke. But he had faith in his nose. Though the gates of the large central archway had not yet been put in place, the archway was stoutly boarded, and Mr. Curtenty could not get through it. He ran along and climbed a rough fence at the side of the manufactory, and so reached the back, which was less securely protected than the front from marauders. The next instant he was in the quadrangle, or "yard" as it is called. And his nose was justified, for he saw smoke meandering furtively, ominously, from a first-floor window. And his eyes detected a faint glow within.

Mr. Curtenty was gloriously alive. The price of Scheele's Acid was nothing to him. He was professionally

Colclough ['koukli] *(Familienname)*
recently ['ri:sntli] *kürzlich, vor kurzem*

---

raze [reiz] *niederreißen*
erection [i'rekʃən] *Errichtung, Bau*
dodge [dɔdʒ] *Kniff*
economic [i:kə'nɔmik] *wirtschaftlich*
test [test] *ausprobieren*
sniff [snif] *schnüffeln, riechen*
purpose ['pə:pəs] *Vorsatz*
trade [treid] *(ausgeübter) Beruf*
profession [prə'feʃən] *Beruf(ung)*
arch-foe ['ɑ:tʃ'fou] *Erzfeind*
indicate ['indikeit] *anzeigen*
unglazed ['ʌn'gleizd] *unverglast*
curl [kə:l] *sich kräuseln*
wisp [wisp] *Fetzen, Streifen*
faith [feiθ] *Vertrauen*
gate [geit] *Torflügel*
archway ['ɑ:tʃwei] *überwölbter Torweg*
stout [staut] *stark, fest*
board [bɔ:d] *mit Brettern verschlagen*
fence [fens] *Zaun*
secure [si'kjuə] *sicher*
protect [prə'tekt] *schützen*
marauder [mə'rɔ:də] *Plünderer*
quadrangle ['kwɔdræŋgl] *viereckiger Gebäudekomplex*
justify ['dʒʌstifai] *rechtfertigen*
meander [mi'ændə] *sich schlängeln*
furtive ['fə:tiv] *heimlich*
ominous ['ɔminəs] *unheilvoll*
detect [di'tekt] *entdecken*
faint [feint] *schwach*
glow [glou] *glühen; Glut*
professional [prə'feʃənl] *beruflich, berufsmäßig*

inspired. He was happy in the midst of calamity and conflagration. He knew the first thing to do and the second thing to do, and did not hesitate a moment. In a quarter of a minute he was in Trafalgar Road again. A policeman, a policeman to take charge! But there was no policeman. But at the corner of the tiny Square, in front of Bleakridge's yellow church, burned a red lamp. Dr. Ackertington's, of course! Mr. Curtenty, forgetting dignity, and yet somehow preserving it, ran to the house and violently rang the bell. He rang it three times with increasing violence.

The door opened.

"'Ere! You're in a 'urry," said a stern, fat, middle-aged maid in cap and apron, as soon as she had satisfied herself that Mr. Curtenty did not belong to the ruling class.

"'Ave ye got th'telephone here?" Mr. Curtenty demanded stiffly.

"And if we have! You can't use it."

"Who wants to use it. You tell your master or missus as Colclough's new pot-bank's afire, and they must telephone for th'fire-brigade." Then he ran off.

Within the quadrangle of the works once more, he descried in the darkness what looked like a mound of sand. He put his hand into it. It was a mound of sand. Seizing one of several buckets which the builder's men had left, he filled it with sand and searched for and found stairs and gingerly mounted them in the black darkness, and guided by his

inspire [in'spaiə] *anregen*
in the midst of [midst] *inmitten*
calamity [kə'læmiti] *Unglück*
conflagration [kɔnflə'greiʃən] *Feuersbrunst*
hesitate ['heziteit] *zögern*
quarter ['kwɔːtə] *Viertel*
take charge [tʃɑːdʒ] *e-e Sache in die Hand nehmen*
tiny ['taini] *winzig*
preserve [pri'zəːv] *bewahren*
violent ['vaiələnt] *heftig*
rang [ræŋ] *läutete*
increase [in'kriːs] *wachsen, zunehmen*
violence ['vaiələns] *Heftigkeit, Ungestüm*
'ere [iə] = here
'urry ['ʌri] = hurry *Eile*
stern [stəːn] *finster, streng*
middle-aged ['midl-'eidʒd] *mittleren Alters*
maid [meid] *(Dienst-) Mädchen*
cap [kæp] *Haube*
apron ['eiprən] *Schürze*
satisfy ['sætisfai] *überzeugen*

'ave [æv] = have
demand [di'mɑːnd] *fragen*
stiff [stif] *steif, formell*
missus *sl.* ['misəs] *gnä' Frau*
pot-bank ['pɔtbæŋk] *Töpferei*
afire [ə'faiə] *in Flammen*
fire-brigade *BE* ['faiəbri'geid] *Feuerwehr*
mound [maund] *Erdwall, -hügel*
seize [siːz] *ergreifen*

bucket ['bʌkit] *Eimer*
search for [səːtʃ] *suchen nach*
gingerly ['dʒindʒəli] *behutsam*
guide [gaid] *leiten, führen*

triumphant nose he passed through a corridor and into a large suffocating room, which room was illuminated by the fire.

Planks of wood were just beginning to crackle. With the sand he smothered their ardour. But there was not enough sand. He descended again, with empty bucket, bungled the stairs, fell, hurt his ankle, swore, limped, got more sand, ascended. After three such ascents he had extinguished the fire and was in darkness. But he had seen enough to decide the origin of the fire. The usual thing! Workmen's negligence. They had been bivouacking in the room, they had made a fire in the grateless hearth—one of your sprawling fires—and they had not put it out on leaving. A few embers had reached a plank leaning at a broad angle against the mantelpiece, had patiently attacked the root of the plank—a slow business, but in the end successful; the plank, deprived of its base, had fallen sideways on to a heap of other planks. And so on. Had not the entire place sweated with damp it might have been a heap of ruins.

Mr. Curtenty, his occupation gone, limped through other corridors and rooms until he saw the light of Trafalgar Road street-lamps through an unglazed window. He looked out, himself unseen. A crowd, small but increasing, was gazing stolidly up at the façade of the works. It could perceive nothing of interest; it had no impulse to do anything; it merely

triumphant [traiˈʌmfənt] *erfolgreich*
suffocate [ˈsʌfəkeit] *ersticken*
illuminate [ilˈjuːmineit] *erleuchten*
plank [plæŋk] *Bohle*
crackle [ˈkrækl] *knistern, prasseln*
smother [ˈsmʌðə] *ersticken*
ardour [ˈɑːdə] *Hitze, Glut*
descend [diˈsend] *hinabsteigen*
bungle [ˈbʌŋgl] *heraufstolpern*
ankle [ˈæŋkl] *(Fuß)Knöchel*
swore [swɔː] *fluchte*
limp [limp] *hinken*
ascend [əˈsend] *hinaufsteigen*
ascent [əˈsent] *Hinaufsteigen*
extinguish [iksˈtiŋgwiʃ] *löschen, ersticken*
negligence [ˈneglidʒəns] *Fahrlässigkeit*
bivouac [ˈbivuæk] *lagern, sich ausruhen*
grateless [ˈgreitlis] *ohne Feuerrost*
hearth [hɑːθ] *Herd, Feuerstelle*
sprawl [sprɔːl] *kriechen, sich ausbreiten*
embers *Pl.* [ˈembəz] *glühende Asche*
angle [ˈæŋgl] *Winkel*
mantelpiece [ˈmæntlpiːs] *Kamineinfassung*
root [ruːt] *unteres Ende*
deprive [diˈpraiv] *berauben*
base [beis] *Unterteil*
heap [hiːp] *Haufen*
entire [inˈtaiə] *ganz*
sweat [swet] *schwitzen, triefen*
damp [dæmp] *Feuchtigkeit*
occupation [ɔkjuˈpeiʃən] *Beschäftigung*
gaze [geiz] *starren*
stolid [ˈstɔlid] *gleichmütig*
perceive [pəˈsiːv] *erkennen*

gazed, in the faint hope of witnessing some terrific catastrophe. Mr. Curtenty continued to look out, proud, patient, invisible, scornful of the crowd.

The expectant crowd in the mire was in due course rewarded by the exciting arrival of a motor-car full of people—Eddie Colclough, a young newly-married wife, and friends. Dr. Ackerington being out, Mrs. Ackerington had telephoned not only to the fire-brigade, but to Eddie, who lived at Cauldon, between Hanbridge and Oldcastle. Mr. and Mrs. Eddie were entertaining at dinner two gentlemen and a lady, and, all being young and adventurous, they had instantly decided to leave dinner and come in a body to the scene of the announced conflagration.

Mr. Curtenty, seeing them and guessing that Mr. Colclough must be among them, went downstairs with pain in his ankle. Eddie, followed by Mrs. Eddie and the others, was in the quadrangle almost before him.

"Where's the fire?" Mr. Colclough demanded fiercely, in bewilderment; he was intensely relieved to see no evidence of a fire, but also—rather illogically—annoyed to see no evidence of a fire.

"It ain't anywhere. I've put it out," answered Mr. Curtenty, coldly, challengingly.

"And who the devil are you, anyway?" cried Mr. Colclough, who was of an aggressive and hasty disposition.

impulse ['impʌls] *Antrieb*

---

witness ['witnis] *Zeuge sein von, miterleben*
terrific [tə'rifik] *schrecklich*
catastrophe [kə'tæstrəfi] *Katastrophe*
scornful ['skɔːnful] *verächtlich*

expectant [iks'pektənt] *erwartungsvoll*
mire ['maiə] *Schlamm, Schmutz*
in due course ['djuː 'kɔːs] *zur rechten Zeit*
reward [ri'wɔːd] *belohnen*
excite [ik'sait] *aufregen*
newly-married ['njuːli 'mærid] *jung verheiratet*
entertain [entə'tein] *bewirten*
adventurous [əd'ventʃərəs] *abenteuerlustig*
instantly ['instəntli] *sofort*
in a body *zusammen*
announce [ə'nauns] *melden*

fierce [fiəs] *heftig, hitzig*
bewilderment [bi'wildəmənt] *Verwirrung*
intensely [in'tensli] *äußerst*
relieve [ri'liːv] *erleichtern*
evidence ['evidəns] *Beweis*
illogical [i'lɔdʒikəl] *unlogisch*
annoyed [ə'nɔid] *ärgerlich*

ain't V [eint] = is not
the devil ['devl] *zum Teufel*
anyway ['eniwei] *überhaupt*
aggressive [ə'gresiv] *streitsüchtig*
hasty ['heisti] *heftig*
disposition [dispə'ziʃən] *Wesen*

"Mr. Curtenty's my name," said Mr. Curtenty, "and if you'll come upstairs I'll show ye a thing or two." His tone gave pause to Mr. Colclough, and at the same time allayed Mr. Colclough's rising suspicion of some hanky-panky in the rumour of the fire.

"Strike a match!" ordered Mr. Colclough at the dark stairs, feeling vainly in his pockets.

"I dunna' smoke," said Mr. Curtenty, grimly.

However, one of the other gentlemen had an electric torch. The six of them stood in the scene of the conflagration and heard Mr. Curtenty's description of the great episode.

The ray of the electric torch lighted Mr. Curtenty's smoke-grimed face. The rest of them—the fashionable aristocracy, including two young and beautiful women—were in shadow. Mr. Curtenty's tale was faultless; it extorted admiration, a little unwilling perhaps at first from Eddie Colclough, but spontaneous enough from the others, and especially from the women.

"Well, here's something for you," said Mr. Colclough, and handed Mr. Curtenty a sovereign.

"Thank ye."

"You must be used to fires," said Mrs. Colclough, smiling warmly.

Mr. Curtenty majestically offered some of his personal history.

"And who are you working for now?" asked Mr. Colclough.

"I'm playing," said Mr. Curtenty.

Mr. Colclough paused.

tone [toun] *Ton*
give pause to [pɔːz] *zum Schweigen bringen*
allay [ə'lei] *beschwichtigen*
suspicion [səs'piʃən] *Argwohn, Verdacht*
hanky-panky ['hæŋki-'pæŋki] *Schwindel*
rumour ['ruːmə] *Gerücht*
strike a match *ein Streichholz anzünden*
vainly ['veinli] *vergeblich*
dunna' ['dʌnə] = do not
grim [grim] *grimmig, wütend*
electric torch [i'lektrik 'tɔːtʃ] *Taschenlampe*
description [dis'kripʃən] *Schilderung*
episode ['episoud] *Ereignis*
ray [rei] *(Licht)Strahl*
smoke-grimed ['smouk-'graimd] *rauchgeschwärzt*
fashionable ['fæʃnəbl] *elegant*
aristocracy [æris'tɔkrəsi] Aristokratie, Oberklasse
shadow ['ʃædou] *Schatten*
tale [teil] *Bericht*
faultless ['fɔːltlis] *einwandfrei*
extort [iks'tɔːt] *abnötigen*
admiration [ædmə'reiʃən] *Bewunderung*
spontaneous [spɔn'teinjəs] *spontan*
sovereign ['sɔvrin] *Sovereign (20-Schilling-Münze)*
be used to [juːst] *gewöhnt sein an*
offer ['ɔfə] *bieten*
personal history ['pəːsnl 'histəri] *Lebensgeschichte*
play [plei] *„herumspielen", nichts tun*
pause [pɔːz] *innehalten*

"What did you say your name was?"

"Mr. Curtenty."

"Well, look here, Curtenty," said Mr. Colclough, and paused again, as though hesitating in his mind.

Mr. Curtenty did not repine at the rough careless omission of the "Mr."; experience had been teaching him.

"Look here, Curtenty. There's no watchman here yet. D'you want a job?"

Mr. Curtenty was engaged on the spot.

Suddenly he hurried from the room. The others followed him. The electric torch lighted him from behind. His ears had been copying the excellent example of his nose. He reached one of the front unglazed windows and put his head through a square. A fire-engine had arrived with an enormous fluster and bluster and glint of brass helmets. A fine effort on the part of the Bursley Fire Brigade—forty minutes!

Mr. Curtenty bawled angrily, disdainfully, to the brigade:

"It's out! Get away wi' yer sprinklin' machane! It's out! I'm telling ye!"

Then he turned and faced the torch.

"You perfect duck!" exclaimed young Mrs. Colclough, and carried away by gratitude for a great deed, and by her youthful sentimentalism—in all her beauty and her finery put her ringed hands on the shoulders of the old man and kissed his sooty plain face.

repine [ri'pain] *murren*
careless ['kɛəlis] *unbekümmert*
experience [iks'piəriəns] *Erfahrung*

engage [in'geidʒ] *an-, einstellen*
spot [spɔt] *Stelle*
hurry ['hʌri] *eilen*
light [lait] *(be)leuchten*
copy ['kɔpi] *nachahmen*
square [skwɛə] *Viereck*
fire-engine ['faiəendʒin] *Feuerspritze*
enormous [i'nɔːməs] *ungeheuer*
fluster ['flʌstə] *Aufregung, Tumult*
bluster ['blʌstə] *Brausen, Lärm*
glint [glint] *Schimmer, Glitzern*
brass [brɑːs] *Messing*
helmet ['helmit] *Helm*
effort F ['efət] *„Leistung"*

bawl [bɔːl] *brüllen*
disdainful [dis'deinful] *geringschätzig*
wi' [wi] = with
yer [jəː] = your
sprinklin' machane = sprinkling machine *Sprengwagen*
face [feis] *das Gesicht zuwenden, ins ... sehen*
duck F [dʌk] *Schätzchen*
gratitude ['grætitjuːd] *Dankbarkeit*
youthful ['juːθful] *jugendlich*
sentimentalism [senti'mentəlizəm] *Rührseligkeit*
finery ['fainəri] *Putz, Staat*
sooty ['suti] *rußig*
plain [plein] *offen, ehrlich*

IV.

In Duck Square there is an establishment which stays open till a late hour nightly, brilliantly lit amid the surrounding gloom. Mr. Curtenty entered this establishment and, pulling a florin from his pocket, bought two plenteous portions of the finest fried fish. He then bought a candle, though candles were not in her line of business, from the white-clad proprietress, who gave him a few matches into the bargain. Then he went across to the fast-closing Dragon Hotel and in the nick of time bought a bottle of beer. Having unlocked the door of the cottage in Woodisun Lane with his own key, he took off his boots at the bottom of the stairs, struck a light, and proceeded upwards, heavily encumbered, into his one-roomed home.

Mrs. Curtenty was fast asleep; the blaze of the candle did not awaken her. His heart was loudly beating. It was the heavenly odour of the fried fish that first caused his wife to dream a delicious dream and then woke her. She saw Mr. Curtenty bending over her, candle in hand.

"Get up, wench," said Mr. Curtenty in a tone so startlingly new and attractive to Mrs. Curtenty that she could not move.

"Jimmy," said she, hopefully, "then us'll go to Harriet's to-morrow?"

"Not me!"

"I shall," said she, sadly. "They'll make me. Aye, lad, I'm going, I am!" She sighed.

nightly ['naitli] *jeden Abend, jede Nacht*
brilliant ['briljənt] *glänzend*
lit [lit] *erleuchtet*
amid [ə'mid] *inmitten*
surround [sə'raund] *umgeben*
gloom [glu:m] *Dunkelheit*
plenteous ['plentjəs] *reichlich*
fry [frai] *braten*
line of business ['biznis] *Branche*
clad [klæd] *gekleidet*
proprietress [prə'praiətris] *Inhaberin*
into the bargain ['bɑ:gin] *als Zugabe*
dragon ['drægən] *Drache*
in the nick of time *gerade zur rechten Zeit*
unlock ['ʌn'lɔk] *aufschließen*
bottom ['bɔtəm] *unteres Ende*
struck [strʌk] *hier: entzündete*
proceed [prə'si:d] *weitergehen*
encumber [in'kʌmbə] *belasten, beladen*
blaze [bleiz] *(Licht-) Schein*
heavenly ['hevnli] *himmlisch*
odour ['oudə] *Duft*
cause [kɔ:s] *veranlassen*
delicious [di'liʃəs] *köstlich*
bend [bend] *sich beugen*

wench [wentʃ] *(Bauern-) Mädchen*
startling ['stɑ:tliŋ] *überraschend*
us'll = we shall
not me *ich nicht*
sad [sæd] *traurig*
make *dazu bringen*
lad [læd] *Junge, Bursche*
sigh [sai] *seufzen*

"I've gotten a job," he shouted. "Get up and set this 'ere fish on a platter."

She raised herself on her elbows and kissed him. Mr. Curtenty felt himself obliged for form's sake to show impatience at the salute.

"'Ere," he grunted. "Thou'rt shaking candle-grease all o'er th'bed."

Nevertheless, he himself adjusted the blanket round his wife's exposed arms and neck.

gotten *(veraltet)* = got
this 'ere fish = this fish here
platter ['plætə] *(Braten-) Platte*
oblige [ə'blaidʒ] *verpflichten*
for form's sake [seik] *der Form halber*
impatience [im'peiʃəns] *Ungeduld*
salute [sə'lu:t] *Begrüßung*
thou'rt ['ðauət] = you are
grunt [grʌnt] *knurren*
candle-grease ['kændlgri:s] *Kerzenwachs*
nevertheless [nevəðə'les] *dennoch*
adjust [ə'dʒʌst] *zurechtlegen*
blanket ['blæŋkit] *Wolldecke*
expose [iks'pouz] *aufdecken, entblößen*

(From: The Woman who stole Everything. London, Cassell & Co.)

Death at 8.30

By C. St. John Sprigg

It was sheer impertinence on the part of X. K. to threaten the Home Secretary himself, for the Home Secretary was a poor man. In any case, even had he been rich enough to pay the exorbitant ransom demanded by X. K. as the price of sparing his life, the Ministerial head of law and order in England could hardly knuckle under to a criminal, however gifted that criminal might be.

Gifted X. K. certainly was. Ten times he had threatened. Seven victims had paid without demur. Three had refused. Three were dead.

Death came to one of the three in the form of a heavy object falling from an attic, found on search by the police, three minutes later, to be empty.

The second man had died from the noiseless puff of a silenced pistol, fired, as it afterwards turned out, from an ambulance that was no ambulance, but a fake.

The third had been incautious enough to think that whisky from a sealed and branded bottle was safe. He died, after about two hours' suffering.

X. K. had by now enough ransom money to satisfy the most extravagant criminal, for each of the seven timorous men had been millionaires, and he had soaked them unmercifully.

sheer [ʃiə] *bloß, rein*
impertinence [im'pəːtinəns] *Unverschämtheit*
on the part of *von seiten*
threaten ['θretn] *bedrohen*
Home Secretary *BE* ['sekrətri] *Innenminister*
exorbitant [ig'zɔːbitənt] *übermäßig, ungeheuer*
ransom ['rænsəm] *Lösegeld*
spare [spɛə] *schonen*
knuckle under to ['nʌkl] *sich beugen*
criminal ['kriminl] *Verbrecher*
gifted ['giftid] *begabt*
victim ['viktim] *Opfer*
demur [di'məː] *Einwand*
refuse [ri'fjuːz] *sich weigern*
attic ['ætik] *Dachgeschoß*
search [səːtʃ] *Durchsuchung*
puff [pʌf] *Rauchwölkchen, leichter Knall*
silenced pistol ['sailənsd 'pistl] *Pistole mit Schalldämpfer*
turn out *sich herausstellen*
ambulance ['æmbjuləns] *Krankenwagen*
fake F [feik] *Schwindel*
incautious [in'kɔːʃəs] *unvorsichtig*
seal [siːl] *versiegeln*
brand [brænd] *mit e-r Schutzmarke versehen*

suffering ['sʌfəriŋ] *Leiden*
timorous ['timərəs] *furchtsam*
soak *sl.* [souk] *j-n schröpfen*
unmerciful [ʌn'məːsiful] *unbarmherzig*

One might have expected X. K. to have ceased his deplorable activities and become an honest and respectable citizen, perhaps giving generously to hospitals, and in due course attaining a knighthood and an honoured grave. But this course did not appeal to him. Or else the detailed and widespread investigations of the police were irritating him. Or else he was actuated by an artist's pride in creation. Or by a spirit of impish mischief. Or by a personal dislike of the Home Secretary—Sir Richard Jauntley.

All these theories were advanced by individual police heads when an excited Home Secretary, trying hard to disguise the nervous quiver in his voice, summoned them to his office by telephone, and showed them the following message, written with the usual X. K. typewriter:

> "£20,000 or you die at 8.30 a.m.G.M.T. on November 13 next. Answer yes (if willing) in The Times personal column, signing yourself 'Sweetheart'. Any attempt to mark the money, or to deviate in any way from the instructions I shall give you for handing it to me, will entail exactly the same penalty as refusal—X.K."

Like all X. K.'s letters, this, by some sublimely impudent trick, was written on Government note-paper and sent, post free, in an O.H.M.S. envelope.

At another time Gooch, who did not get on with his temporary head, might have laughed at X. K.'s nerve.

cease [siːz] *aufhören (mit)*
deplorable [diˈplɔːrəbl] *erbärmlich*
in due course [djuː] *zu gegebener Zeit*
attain [əˈtein] *erlangen*
knighthood [ˈnaithud] *Ritterwürde*
honoured grave [ˈɔnəd ˈgreiv] *ehrenhaftes Begräbnis*
appeal [əˈpiːl] *gefallen*
detailed [ˈditeild] *genau*
widespread [ˈwaidspred] *ausgedehnt*
investigation [investiˈgeiʃən] *Nachforschung*
irritate [ˈiriteit] *reizen*
actuate [ˈæktjueit] *antreiben*
artist [ˈɑːtist] *Künstler*
creation [kriˈeiʃən] *Schöpfung*
impish [ˈimpiʃ] *boshaft*
mischief [ˈmistʃif] *Mutwille*
advance [ədˈvɑːns] *vorbringen*
head [hed] *Führer, Chef*
disguise [disˈgaiz] *verbergen*
quiver [ˈkwivə] *zittern*
summon [ˈsʌmən] *herbeizitieren*
a. m. = ante meridiem *vormittags*
G. M. T. = Greenwich Mean Time *mittlere Greenwich-Zeit*
personal column [ˈkɔləm] *Familienanzeigen*
deviate [ˈdiːvieit] *abweichen*
entail [inˈteil] *zur Folge haben*
penalty [ˈpenlti] *Strafe*
refusal [riˈfjuːzəl] *Weigerung*
sublime [səˈblaim] *großartig*
impudent [ˈimpjudənt] *unverschämt*
note-paper [ˈnoutpeipə] *Briefpapier*
post free *portofrei*

Jauntley was nobody's sweetheart, not at the tautest stretch of an overheated imagination.

Jauntley pulled angrily at a ragged white moustache and turned to Paule, Gooch's colleague.

"Damned inefficiency! There's no other word for it. Here's this man. Laughs at us! Threatens me! Me!"

"And he's always done what he's threatened, hitherto," said Hamerton, the third member of the conference and of the so-called "Triumvirate" which ruled the reorganized C.I.D.

Jauntley paled again at this reminder of the nature of the menace. "What do you suggest?" he asked irritably. "That we should give in to him?"

"Good heavens, no, sir!" said Hamerton, his almost Oriental face, with its melancholy whiskers, showing a faint trace of amusement at his Chief's jumpiness. I think he's gone too far this time. He's given a date; an exact time. He's never done that before. The thing is for you, sir, to be put at that time in an obvious sort of place, a tempting place, where X. K. can get in, but can't get out again. A trap, in fact."

"I mean metaphorically, of course," he added, seeing that his remark might otherwise suggest some monster patent mouse-trap with Sir Richard as the dangling and helpless bait.

And indeed it did evoke some such image in his hearer, for Jauntley snorted.

O.H.M.S. = On His Majesty's Service *Dienst..., dienstlich*
temporary ['tempərəri] *zeitweilig*
nerve [nəːv] *Mut*

---

taut [tɔːt] *straff, angespannt*
stretch of imagination [imædʒi'neiʃən] *Aufbietung aller Phantasie*
ragged ['rægid] *zottig*
moustache [məs'tɑːʃ] *Schnurrbart*
inefficiency [ini'fiʃənsi] *Unfähigkeit*
hitherto ['hiðə'tuː] *bisher*
triumvirate [trai'ʌmvirit] *Triumvirat, Dreigestirn*
C.I.D. = Criminal Investigation Department *(britische Kriminalpolizei)*
pale [peil] *erbleichen*
reminder [ri'maində] *Mahnung, Erinnerung*
menace ['menəs] *Drohung*
suggest [sə'dʒest] *vorschlagen, nahelegen*
irritable ['iritəbl] *gereizt*
good heavens! *Pl.* ['hevnz] *du lieber Himmel!*
whiskers *Pl.* ['wiskəz] *Backenbart*
faint [feint] *schwach*
trace [treis] *Spur*
jumpiness ['dʒʌmpinis] *Nervosität*
tempting ['temptiŋ] *verlockend*
trap [træp] *Falle*
metaphorical [metə'fɔrikəl] *bildlich*
monster ['mɔnstə] *Riesen ...*
dangle ['dæŋgl] *baumeln*
bait [beit] *Köder*
evoke [i'vouk] *hervorrufen*
image ['imidʒ] *Bild*
snort [snɔːt] *schnauben*

"Oh, I'm to be the tethered goat for the tiger, am I? No, thank you! X. K. says I'm to be killed at a certain date and time. Right, I survive it. Public confidence rises! Our job's done! Instead of this nonsense of putting me where he can get at me, make me absolutely inaccessible."

Paule had up till now ventured no suggestion. Now he spoke, his young, student's face thoughtful behind the thick-lensed spectacles. "Supposing this exact time business is all bluff? It may be intended only to put us off our guard before and after the time mentioned."

"That has to be considered," admitted Gooch. "So from this moment Sir Richard must be strictly guarded."

"And I must ask you, sir," he added, turning his huge red moon-face to the Chief, "not to touch any food or drink without consulting the expert we shall put at your disposal. None the less, my personal opinion still is that X. K. will strain every nerve to fulfil his promise to the letter."

"An aeroplane," suddenly exclaimed Sir Richard, whose mind, neglecting unimportant details, had been working at high pressure on X.K.-proof refuges.

Hamerton shook his head mournfully. "Very risky. He might tamper with the structure. Or go up in another aeroplane with a machine-gun. No, you stay on the ground, sir, where we can keep an eye on you!"

"A submarine," suggested Sir Richard, with less confidence.

tether ['teðə] *anbinden*
goat [gout] *Ziege*
survive [sə'vaiv] *überleben*
public confidence ['pʌblik 'kɔnfidens] *Vertrauen der Öffentlichkeit*
inaccessible [inæk'sesəbl] *unerreichbar*
venture ['ventʃə] *sich erlauben*
suggestion [sə'dʒestʃən] *Vorschlag*
thick-lensed [lenzd] *mit dicken Gläsern*
student ['stjuːdənt] *Gelehrter*
spectacles *Pl.* ['spektəklz] *Brille*
supposing [sə'pouziŋ] *angenommen*
bluff [blʌf] *Irreführung*
intend [in'tend] *beabsichtigen*
put s. b. off his guard [gaːd] *j-n unachtsam werden lassen*
mention ['menʃən] *erwähnen*
consider [kən'sidə] *berücksichtigen*
admit [əd'mit] *zugeben*
guard [gaːd] *bewachen*
consult [kən'sʌlt] *befragen*
put s. th. at s. b.'s disposal [dis'pouzəl] *j-m etwas zur Verfügung stellen*
none the less [nʌn] *nichtsdestoweniger*
opinion [ə'pinjən] *Meinung*
strain [strein] *anspannen*
neglect [ni'glekt] *vernachlässigen*
X. K.-proof [pruːf] *vor X. K. sicher*
refuge ['refjuːdʒ] *Zuflucht*
mournful ['mɔːnful] *traurig*
risky ['riski] *gefährlich*
tamper ['tæmpə] *sich zu schaffen machen*
submarine [sʌbmə'riːn] *U-Boot*

Gooch made a clicking noise. "Dreadfully vulnerable! He'd just torpedo you. Or send down a diver. Remember the fellow's ingenuity."

This discussion proceeded for some time on these lines. The three police officials had suffered a good deal of unmerited criticism during their conduct of the X. K. investigation in the past; and they could not help getting a certain malicious pleasure now from their superior's evident funk, nor even refrain from augmenting it by pointing out flaws in his desperate expedients. Even his scheme of having a hole cut in a cliff face and being walled up in it for a day had objections.

"A whiff of poison gas through a tube," suggested Hamerton, casually running a lean brown hand through his drooping whiskers; and Sir Richard went pale.

"Or he might slip in the hiding-place just before you did," said Gooch, with a barely perceptible wink at Paule, and the Home Secretary found this prospect even more distressing. Alone with X. K. for a day!

It must not, however, be supposed that three high police officials were unequal to the task of guarding Sir Richard Jauntley against the most far-fetched machinations of X. K. When he had exhausted his fantastic expedients, and was prepared to listen to sense, they put their heads together and worked out a satisfying plan.

click [klik] *klicken, schnalzen*
vulnerable ['vʌlnərəbl] *verwund-, angreifbar*
torpedo [tɔː'piːdou] *torpedieren*
diver ['daivə] *Taucher*
ingenuity [indʒi'njuːiti] *Geschicklichkeit*
proceed [prə'siːd] *vorangehen*
on these lines *auf diese Weise*
unmerited ['ʌn'meritid] *unverdient*
criticism ['kritisizəm] *Kritik*
conduct ['kɔndəkt] *Führung*
malicious [mə'liʃəs] *boshaft*
superior [sjuː'piəriə] *Vorgesetzte(r)*
funk *sl.* [fʌŋk] *„Bammel", Angst*
refrain [ri'frein] *unterlassen*
augment [ɔːg'ment] *vergrößern*
flaw [flɔː] *Fehler*
desperate ['despərit] *verzweifelt*
expedient [iks'piːdjənt] *Ausweg*
scheme [skiːm] *Plan*
hole [houl] *Loch*
cliff face *Vorderseite eines Felsens*
wall up *einmauern*
objection [əb'dʒekʃən] *Bedenken*
whiff [wif] *Hauch, Schuß*
poison ['pɔizn] *Gift*
tube [tjuːb] *Röhre*
casual ['kæʒjuəl] *nachlässig*
lean [liːn] *mager*
droop ['druːp] *herabhängen*
barely ['bɛəli] *kaum*
perceptible [pə'septəbl] *wahrnehmbar*
wink [wiŋk] *Zwinkern*
prospect ['prɔspekt] *Aussicht*
distressing [dis'tresiŋ] *betrüblich*

The vaults of the Bank of England were put at their disposal. In a central vault were arranged three chairs, in which would sit Gooch, Paule and Hamerton—and no one else. Each was to be armed. In the middle of the vault, their chairs ranged round it, they placed a structure which had been specially completed for the occasion. It consisted of a cell of thick bullet-proof glass, locked according to a combination known fully only to Sir Richard Jauntley.

Gooch, Hamerton and Paule each knew two letters of the six-cipher combination, and, therefore, their united knowledge was necessary to open it. It will be seen from this fact that the men involved had not even flinched from the possibility that one among them might be X. K., a circumstance that had some justification in X. K.'s surprising knowledge.

The Home Secretary was to sit inside this glass cube, a revolver in his hand. Mindful of Hamerton's suggestion of poison gas, the cell was ventilated into the vault by a filtering apparatus, so that even if the whole vault were filled with poison gas, Sir Richard would still escape.

The events on the fatal day were as follows. At 6 a.m. six police experts, assisted by architects, inspected the central vault and all communicating and adjacent rooms and passages. They searched the bare massive structure for concealed weapons, unexplained pipes or wires, or any other body unaccounted for. In view of the guard normally stationed

suppose [sə'pouz] *annehmen*
unequal ['ʌn'iːkwəl] *nicht gewachsen*
far-fetched ['fɑː'fetʃt] *weit hergeholt, ausgeklügelt*
machination [mæki'neiʃən] *Machenschaft*
exhaust [ig'zɔːst] *erschöpfen*
sense [sens] *Vernunft*

---

vault [vɔːlt] *Gewölbe*
arm [ɑːm] *bewaffnen*
range [reindʒ] *in Reihen aufstellen*
complete [kəm'pliːt] *herrichten*
occasion [ə'keiʒən] *Gelegenheit*
bullet-proof ['bulitpruːf] *kugelsicher*
lock [lɔk] *(ver)schließen*
six-cipher ['saifə] *sechsziffrig*
involved [in'vɔlvd] *beteiligt*
flinch [flintʃ] *ausweichen*
justification [dʒʌstifi'keiʃən] *Rechtfertigung*
cube [kjuːb] *Würfel*
mindful ['maindful] *eingedenk*
suggestion [sə'dʒestʃən] *Hinweis*
ventilate ['ventileit] *entlüften*
filtering apparatus [æpə'reitəs] *Filtervorrichtung*
escape [is'keip] *entkommen*
event [i'vent] *Ereignis*
inspect [in'spekt] *untersuchen*
communicate [kə'mjuːnikeit] *in Verbindung stehen*
adjacent [ə'dʒeisənt] *angrenzend*
bare [bɛə] *kahl, bloß*
conceal [kən'siːl] *verstecken*
weapon ['wepən] *Waffe*
unexplained ['ʌniks'pleind] *unerklärlich*

at the Bank, and the precautions always taken in connection with the vaults, the existence of any sinister apparatus was in the highest degree unlikely, and none was, in fact, found.

Having been given the all-clear, three cordons were formed round the vault. The two inner cordons were men from the Yard, aided by picked Bank officials. The outer cordon was formed by armed guardsmen.

Each cordon could only pass visitors through a door having a lock set for the occasion to a combination known in whole only to Sir Richard Jauntley, but divided among Paule, Hamerton and Gooch, and also among the three senior officers in each cordon.

At eight o'clock on the morning of November 13th, an armoured car pulled up at the Bank. No whisper of the threat to the Home Secretary had been allowed to reach the public, and so its arrival was hardly noticed.

Sir Richard and his three companions passed slowly through the cordons. In each case they were not only carefully scrutinized by the three senior officials of each cordon, but their finger-prints were compared with a chart to make sure there was no impersonation. All these precautions gave a reassuring sense of security to the Home Secretary, who had, up till then, felt unpleasantly like a condemned murderer awaiting a doubtful reprieve.

wire ['waiə] *Draht*
body ['bɔdi] *Gegenstand*
unaccounted ['ʌnə'kauntid] *seltsam*
in view of [vjuː] *angesichts*
guard [gaːd] *Wache*
station ['steiʃən] *postieren*

precaution [pri'kɔːʃən] *Vorsichtsmaßregel*
sinister [si'nistə] *unheimlich*
unlikely [ʌn'laikli] *unwahrscheinlich*
all-clear ['ɔl'kliə] *alles in Ordnung, Genehmigung*
cordon ['kɔːdn] *Postenkette*
Yard = Scotland Yard ['skɔtlənd 'jaːd] *(Sitz der) Londoner Kriminalpolizei*
pick [pik] *auswählen*
guardsman ['gaːdzmən] *Wächter*
pass [paːs] *durchlassen*
a lock set for the occasion *ein für diese Gelegenheit eingestelltes Schloß*
in whole *im ganzen*
senior ['siːnjə] *ranghöher*
armoured ['aːməd] *Panzer . . .*
pull up *vorfahren*
whisper ['wispə] *Geflüster, Getuschel*
threat [θret] *Bedrohung*
arrival [ə'raivəl] *Ankunft*
hardly ['haːdli] *kaum*
companion [kəm'pænjən] *Gefährte*
scrutinize ['skruːtinaiz] *überprüfen*
finger-print [print] *Fingerabdruck*
compare [kəm'pɛə] *vergleichen*
chart [tʃaːt] *Karte, Tabelle*
impersonation [impəːsə'neiʃən] *Personenverwechslung*
reassure [riːə'ʃuə] *beruhigen*

The last massive door clanged to behind them. Sir Richard got into his glass cube and sat there awkwardly, feeling ridiculously like a fish in an aquarium. The three police heads sat round him, silent, each with a revolver on his knees. Sir Richard picked up his, looked at it, and put it down again. Then he looked at his watch. It was 8.10. Twenty minutes to go.

A cough from Gooch echoed hollowly. Except for the chairs and the glass cube, the vault was bare, and lit only by the steady glow from the naked light bulbs, set in the roof, behind metal guards.

The four men were buried deep in the soil. It was utterly impossible for any visitor from the outside world to reach them. A flood, a revolution, or another Fire of London, would all pass unnoticed over their heads. Anyone trying to sap his way to them would encounter cement, iron plates, granite, and even water.

All four men began to feel a little foolish. What a massive defence they had devised to ward off the feeble powers of a pseudonymous brigand!

At 8.29 Sir Richard Jauntley glanced at his wrist-watch and smiled. He made some gesture of contempt, and his lips moved, but of course they could not hear him through the glass. Quite suddenly his smile changed to a grimace of pain; his whole face contorted. He got up, flung out his arms wildly, and writhed on the floor. He twitched violently twice, and then was still.

sense [sens] *Gefühl*
condemn [kən'dem] *verurteilen*
doubtful ['dautful] *zweifelhaft*
reprieve [ri'pri:v] *Gnadenfrist*

---

clang [klæŋ] *klirren, schmettern*
awkward ['ɔ:kwəd] *unbeholfen*
ridiculous [ri'dikjuləs] *lächerlich*
pick up *aufnehmen*
twenty minutes to go *noch zwanzig Minuten*
cough [kɔf] *Husten*
echo ['ekou] *widerhallen*
hollow ['hɔlou] *hohl*
except for [ik'sept] *bis auf*
lit [lit] *erleuchtet*
steady ['stedi] *gleichmäßig*
glow [glou] *Leuchten*
bulb [bʌlb] *Glühbirne*
guard [gɑ:d] *Schutzgitter*
bury ['beri] *begraben*
soil [sɔil] *Erde*
utterly ['ʌtəli] *völlig*
flood [flʌd] *Flut*
Fire of London *Feuersbrunst in London (1666)*
unnoticed ['ʌn'noutist] *unbemerkt*
sap [sæp] *graben*
encounter [in'kauntə] *treffen auf*
foolish ['fu:liʃ] *dumm, albern*
defence [di'fens] *Verteidigung*
devise [di'vaiz] *ausdenken*
ward off [wɔ:d] *abwehren*
feeble ['fi:bl] *schwach*
pseudonymous [psju:'dɔniməs] *pseudonym, unbekannt*
brigand ['brigənd] *Räuber*
wrist-watch ['ristwɔtʃ] Armbanduhr
gesture ['dʒestʃə] *Geste*

When they got to him he was stone-dead.

Well, there it was. X. K. had succeeded beyond all hope. And presently, as the three men knew, the Press would be carrying a message of terror which would make every future exaction of X. K. easy. So easy that his victims would be afraid even to report the matter to the police, afraid to do anything but pay up at once.

There was no sign of anything lethal in the glass cube. They could not associate the symptoms with any known poison—no drifting odour of almonds, such as is left by hydrocyanic acid, none of the acute agonies and foam-flecked lips of strychnine.

There was no wound upon him.

Their examination was made hurriedly. The police surgeon could go into the details.

"Well, we're beaten, for the moment," said Hamerton grimly. We must have Sir Charles Martell for the post-mortem."

Gooch was looking several years older. "Poor old Jauntley," he said, his moon-face pale. "To think I laughed at him for being in a funk! Only an hour or two ago."

"Pull yourself together, old chap!" replied Hamerton, with the coldness of the expert who sees nothing but his job. "Here's a problem. Don't think of anything else. It's a tough problem, but we must solve it."

"Well, I must leave that to you for the moment. I shall be spending the next twenty-four hours being

contempt [kən'tempt] *Verachtung*
contort [kən'tɔːt] *sich verzerren*
flung out [flʌŋ] *(plötzlich) ausstrecken*
writhe [raið] *sich krümmen*
twitch [twitʃ] *zucken*
violent [vaiələnt] *heftig*

---

stone-dead ['stoun'ded] *mausetot*
succeed [sək'siːd] *Erfolg haben*
presently ['prezṅtli] *alsbald*
carry a message ['mesidʒ] *Nachricht bringen*
exaction [ig'zækʃən] *Erpressung*
be afraid [ə'freid] *sich fürchten*
report [ri'pɔːt] *anzeigen*
pay up *voll bezahlen*
lethal ['liːθəl] *tödlich*
associate [ə'souʃieit] *in Verbindung bringen*
symptom ['simptəm] *Symptom, Anzeichen*
drift [drift] *strömen*
odour ['oudə] *Geruch*
almond ['ɑːmənd] *Mandel*
hydrocyanic acid ['haidrousai'ænik 'æsid] *Blausäure*
acute [ə'kjuːt] *heftig*
agony ['ægəni] *Qual, Todeskampf*
foam-flecked ['foum'flekt] *schaumbedeckt*
strychnine ['strikniːn] *Strychnin*
wound [wuːnd] *Wunde*
examination [igzæmi'neiʃən] *Untersuchung*
hurried ['hʌrid] *eilig*
surgeon ['səːdʒən] *Arzt*
detail ['diteil] *Einzelheit*
beaten ['biːtn] *geschlagen*
grim [grim] *wütend*
post-mortem ['poust'mɔːtəm] *Leichenöffnung*
chap [tʃæp] *Bursche, Junge*
tough [tʌf] *schwierig*
solve [sɔlv] *lösen*

badgered by Cabinet committees," said Gooch.

Paule took off his glasses and polished them thoughtfully. It was the first really big problem, as he understood it, that he had been called upon to face. He was only thirty-two, and his rise in the C.I.D. had been meteoric. He had been pitchforked into it by old Lord Goolmouth, with no qualifications except a University degree and a telling analysis of a much-reported crime which he had made casually at a dinner at a house-party of Lord Goolmouth's. The point was that the police had happened to be wrong, and Paule's analysis, pointing to an apparently innocent witness as the murderer, had happened to be right. Everyone had thought at first that Goolmouth was in his dotage. But Paule had risen like a comet. His talent for organization, oddly enough, and not any brilliant solutions, had been the main cause of his progress. His keen analytic mind certainly had been useful from time to time, but in seven years it had never once been presented with a really first class problem.

Now it had, and he wondered if, in the lapse of years spent in routine, it had grown a little rusty. He replaced his glasses with a sigh. Impossible to do anything until the surgeon had done his work.

Late that afternoon Paule accompanied Hamerton into the room in which Sir Charles was busy over his gruesome task. The naked body on

spend [spend] *verbringen*
badger ['bædʒə] *plagen, hetzen*
committee [kə'miti] *Ausschuß*

---

polish ['pɔliʃ] *putzen*
thoughtful ['θɔːtful] *nachdenklich*
call upon *auffordern*
face [feis] *ins Gesicht sehen, entgegentreten*
meteoric [miːti'ɔrik] *meteorhaft, glänzend*
pitchfork ['pitʃfɔːk] *drängen*
qualification [kwɔlifi'keiʃən] *Befähigung*
university degree [juːni'vəsiti di'griː] *akademischer Grad*
telling ['teliŋ] *eindrucksvoll*
analysis [ə'næləsis] *gründliche Untersuchung*
casual ['kæʒjuəl] *gelegentlich*
happen to be wrong *zufällig unrecht haben*
apparent [ə'pærənt] *offenbar*
innocent ['inəsnt] *unschuldig*
witness ['witnis] *Zeuge*
dotage ['doutidʒ] *Altersschwachsinn*
odd [ɔd] *seltsam*
brilliant ['briljənt] *glänzend, geistreich*
solution [sə'luːʃən] *Lösung*
main [mein] *Haupt . . .*
cause [kɔːs] *Ursache*
progress ['prougres] *Aufstieg*
keen [kiːn] *scharf*
it had not been presented with [pri'zentid] *ihm war nicht vorgelegt worden*
lapse [læps] *Verlauf*
routine [ruː'tiːn] *mechanische Arbeit*
grow rusty ['rʌsti] *einrosten*
replace [ri'pleis] *wieder aufsetzen*

the slab, with its pathetic heap of clothes and neatly ranged personal effects nearby, was too familiar to cause either of them much uneasiness.

Sir Charles hummed gently to himself, as was his wont during post-mortems, and there was an occasional clink and splash of an instrument dropped in a glass beaker. The air was heavy with the pungent aroma of formalin.

"Found anything, Sir Charles?"

"Oh, yes, simple enough! I spotted it at once. He's been killed with my poison!"

"Your poison!" exclaimed Hamerton, his hand dropping from his whiskers.

Sir Charles rubbed his chin with a quizzical smile. "Yes, mine. Mind you, I hardly regarded it as a poison when I discovered it. It is a medicine. T. T. 1, I christened it in the article I wrote on it, but my colleagues insist on calling it Martellin. Well, well, I suppose it might have a worse name! And to think poor old Jauntley succumbed to it. Why only yesterday in the 'Athenæum'—" Sir Charles' garrulousness was his only fault, and Paule interrupted him.

"How do you mean it's a medicine?"

"It is a stimulant to the heart and the central nervous system. But of course if the heart is over-stimulated—complete and instant collapse. That's what happened here."

"And what is a fatal dose?"

sigh [sai] *Seufzer*
accompany [ə'kʌmpəni] *begleiten*
gruesome ['gru:səm] *grausig*

---

slab [slæb] *Steinplatte, Fliese*
pathetic [pə'θetik] *rührend*
heap [hi:p] *Haufen*
neat [ni:t] *sauber, ordentlich*
effects *Pl.* [i'fekts] *Habseligkeiten*
familiar [fə'miljə] *vertraut*
cause [kɔ:s] *verursachen*
uneasiness [ʌn'i:zinis] *Unbehagen*
hum [hʌm] *summen*
gentle [dʒentl] *leise*
wont [wount] *Gewohnheit*
clink [kliŋk] *Klirren*
splash [splæʃ] *Platschen*
beaker ['bi:kə] *Becherglas*
pungent ['pʌndʒənt] *scharf, stechend*
aroma [ə'roumə] *Aroma, Duft*
formalin ['fɔ:məlin] *Formalin*
spot F [spɔt] *erkennen*
at once [wʌns] *sofort*
exclaim [iks'kleim] *ausrufen*
quizzical ['kwizikəl] *spöttisch*
mind you *wohlgemerkt*
discover [dis'kʌvə] *entdecken*
medicine ['medsin] *Medizin*
christen ['krisn] *taufen*
colleague ['kɔli:g] *Kollege*
insist on [in'sist] *bestehen auf*
succumb [sə'kʌm] *erliegen*
garrulousness ['gæruləsnis] *Schwatzhaftigkeit*
fault [fɔ:lt] *Fehler*
interrupt [intə'rʌpt] *unterbrechen*

"Well, there is the pure extract, such as I experimented with, and the highly dilute form in which it would be supplied for hospital use."

"I mean in the pure extract?"

"An ox was killed," said Sir Charles slowly, "with a dose which consisted of one cubic millimetre of water, in which the pure extract was dilute in the proportion of 10,000 parts to one."

"Sounds a lot," said Hamerton vaguely.

Paule, whose mathematical training grasped precisely at this figure, stared. "But, good heavens! Such a dose would be almost invisible!"

"Exactly," replied Sir Charles affably.

"But—is it possible?"

Sir Charles smiled. "I see you are unfamiliar with the literature of the endocrine glands. Pure extracts of their basic secretions act violently on the system even in microscopic doses. Martellin is an extract from the pineal gland—an organ hidden by the convolutions of the cerebrum."

"But how could this devil have got hold of it!" exclaimed Hamerton.

"Unfortunately I described its preparation, which is reasonably simple, in the columns of 'Nature'", admitted Sir Charles. "I did not, of course, appreciate the possibility of its use as a poison. Our friend is evidently a well-read man. The odd thing is, I believe I am the only man who could have guessed that Jauntley did not die from natural causes. The symptoms of Martellin poisoning are

stimulant ['stimjulənt] *Anregungsmittel*
central nervous system ['sentrəl 'nə:vəs 'sistim] *Zentralnervensystem*
stimulate ['stimjuleit] *anregen*
nstant ['instənt] *sofortig*
collapse [kə'læps] *Kollaps, Zusammenbruch*
dose [dous] *Dosis*

---

pure [pjuə] *rein*
extract [iks'trækt] *Extrakt*
experiment [iks'perimənt] *experimentieren*
dilute [dail'ju:t] *verdünnen; verdünnt*
supply [sə'plai] *liefern*
consist of [kən'sist] *bestehen aus*
cubic millimetre ['kju:bik 'milimi:tə] *Kubikmillimeter*
proportion [prə'pɔ:ʃən] *Verhältnis*
sound [saund] *klingen, sich anhören*
grasp at [gra:sp] *greifen nach*
precise [pri'sais] *genau*
figure ['figə] Zahl
invisible [in'vizəbl] *unsichtbar*
affable ['æfəbl] *leutselig, freundlich*
unfamiliar ['ʌnfə'miljə] *nicht vertraut*
endocrine gland ['endoukrain 'glænd] *Drüse mit innerer Sekretion*
secretion [si'kri:ʃən] *Sekretion, Absonderung*
microscopic [maikrəs'kɔpik] *mikroskopisch*
pineal gland ['painiəl] *Zirbeldrüse*
convolution [kɔnvə'lu:ʃən] *Windung*
cerebrum ['seribrəm] *Großhirn*
get hold of [hould] *in die Hände bekommen*
preparation [prepə'reiʃən] *Herstellung*
reasonably ['ri:znəbli] *ziemlich*

absolutely undistinguishable from those of collapse due to syncope, except that the Martellin also stimulates the suprarenal glands, which discharge a quantity of adrenalin into the bloodstream. I did not mention this fact in my article, and in the ordinary way no pathologist would think of testing the bloodstream of a syncope victim for excess adrenalin. In spite of his cleverness, therefore, your man never guessed that the one man who could detect his crime would examine the body. That at last shows he is liable to error."

"Wasn't the article signed with your name?"

Sir Charles shook his head. "No. With my pseudonym 'Hormone'. I have contributed to the medical press so often under that pseudonym that any medical man would know who 'Hormone' was, but a mere layman would probably not associate it with the Home Office pathologist."

Paule was pacing up and down the room, lost in thought. His moods of abstraction, frequent enough, marked him as a dreamer, even if a successful dreamer. His absent-mindedness had sometimes caused inconvenience, but his colleagues had grown resigned to these fits of reverie, and waited only for the flashing glimpses of intuition which sometimes–not always–lightened them.

"How would it be administered, Sir Charles?" went on Hamerton.

The surgeon stirred a beaker of boiling water reflectively. "By the

column ['kɔləm] *Spalte*
appreciate [ə'pri:ʃieit] *erkennen*
well-read ['wel'red] (sehr) belesen
guess [ges] *vermuten*

---

undistinguishable ['ʌndis'tiŋgwiʃəbl] *nicht unterscheidbar*
syncope ['siŋkəpi] *tiefe Ohnmacht*
suprarenal ['sju:prə'ri:nl] *suprarenal, oberhalb der Niere liegend*
discharge [dis'tʃɑ:dʒ] *absondern*
adrenalin [ə'drenəlin] *Adrenalin (Nebennierenhormon)*
bloodstream ['blʌdstri:m] *Blut(kreislauf)*
pathologist [pə'θɔlədʒist] Pathologe
excess [ik'ses] *Überschuß an*
cleverness ['klevənis] *Klugheit*
detect [di'tekt] *aufdecken*
examine [ig'zæmin] *untersuchen*
be liable ['laiəbl] *unterworfen sein*
error ['erə] *Irrtum*
pseudonym ['psju:dənim] *Deckname*
contribute [kən'tribju:t] *beitragen*
medical man F ['medikəl] *„Doktor", Arzt*
mere [miə] *bloß*
layman ['leimən] *Laie*
Home Office *BE* ['ɔfis] *Innenministerium*
pace [peis] *schreiten*
mood [mu:d] *Stimmung*
abstraction [æb'strækʃən] *Zerstreutheit, Versunkenheit*
mark [mɑ:k] *kennzeichnen*
absent-mindedness ['æbsent'maindidnis] *Geistesabwesenheit*
inconvenience [inkən'vi:njəns] *Ungelegenheit*

mouth. Or intravenous injection. The injection would be more rapid in its effects."

"But how could it be done?" asked Hamerton helplessly, "so that he would die at a fixed time. How long does the stuff take to act?"

"Ten seconds, say, if administered by the mouth. Practically at once if given intravenously."

"Then how was it done?"

"That's your job," said Sir Charles cruelly. Then relenting: "Well, one idea does occur to me—a capsule with a specially tough wall, with a fatal dose inside in a dilute form. Until the wall of the capsule was digested, the drug wouldn't act."

"Of course!" said Hamerton with relief. "He was poisoned before he got to the Bank!"

Paule suddenly woke up from his abstraction. "Poisoned before he got to the Bank?"

"Yes. X. K. could have worked out the exact time a capsule would have taken to digest, and administered it beforehand, so that Jauntley died at 8.30 exactly."

Paule shook his head. "I don't think that's possible; is it, Sir Charles? Not to fix the time to the minute—or the second as it was in this case!"

"Quite impossible, for the exact lapse of time depends on unknown factors. The rate of secretion of the gastric juices, for instance, vary from hour to hour in every subject. One would have to allow a possible

resigned [ri'zaind] *ergeben*
fit [fit] *Anfall*
reverie ['revəri] *Träumerei*
flash [flæʃ] *aufblitzen*
glimpse [glimps] *Lichtblick*
intuition [intju:'iʃən] *Erkenntnis*
lighten ['laitn] *erleuchten*
administer [əd'ministə] *verabreichen*
reflective [ri'flektiv] *nachdenklich*

---

intravenous [intrə'vi:nəs] *intravenös, in die Vene*
injection [in'dʒekʃən] *Injektion, Einspritzung*
fix [fiks] *festlegen*
stuff F [stʌf] *„Zeug"*
practical ['præktikəl] *praktisch*
at once [wʌns] *sofort*
cruel ['kruəl] *hart, grausam*
relent [ri'lent] *einlenken*
occur [ə'kə:] *einfallen*
capsule ['kæpsju:l] *Kapsel*
tough [tʌf] *zäh, fest*
digest [di'dʒest] *verdauen; sich auflösen*
drug [drʌg] *Droge, Medikament*
relief [ri'li:f] *Erleichterung*
work out *ausrechnen*
exact [ig'zækt] *genau*
beforehand [bi'fɔ:hænd] *vorher*
case [keis] *Fall*
lapse [læps] *Verlauf*
depend on [di'pend] *abhängen von*
rate [reit] *Quote; Geschwindigkeit*
gastric juice ['gæstrik 'dʒu:s] *Magensaft*
vary ['vɛəri] *schwanken*
subject ['sʌbdʒikt] *Person*
allow [ə'lau] *rechnen mit*

error of ten minutes, or a quarter of an hour, each way."

"Anyway," added Paule, "Briggs and Thomson are here, so that we could check the matter with them."

Hamerton sent for the two constables to whom had been given the task of guarding Jauntley until his arrival at the Bank.

"Briggs, we have reason to believe that Sir Richard Jauntley took some form of capsule or pilule on the morning of his death. Is that possible?"

Briggs thought carefully.

"I should say it is impossible, sir," he said at last. "As you know, we were on guard in his room all night, and he certainly took nothing then."

"Perhaps he used to carry a box of medicine in his clothes, and the poison was substituted for one?"

"No, sir. It occured to us that X. K. might conceal an explosive or something in Sir Richard's clothes, so as each article was handed to us by his valet, we went through the pockets and checked the contents with Sir Richard. There were no medicines of any kind."

"Perhaps it was concealed in his breakfast? In a piece of bread?"

"Sir Richard had nothing but a cup of coffee, sir. He was going to take his breakfast afterwards."

"Very good, Briggs."

Hamerton ruffled his iron-grey hair, his almost Oriental passivity momentarily disturbed. "I shall believe in magic in a moment!"

anyway ['eniwei] *jedenfalls*

check [tʃek] *nachprüfen*

constable ['kʌnstəbl] *Polizist*

guard [gɑːd] *bewachen*

reason ['riːzn] *Grund*

pilule ['piljuːl] *kleine Pille*

he used to [juːst] *er pflegte zu ..., er ... immer*

substitute ['sʌbstitjuːt] *austauschen*

conceal [kən'siːl] *verbergen*

explosive [iks'plousiv] *Sprengstoff*

article ['ɑːtikl] *hier: Kleidungsstück*

valet ['vælit] *Diener*

go through *durchsuchen*

contents *Pl.* ['kɔntents] *Inhalt*

but *außer*

ruffle ['rʌfl] *durcheinanderbringen, zerwühlen*

iron ['aiən] *Eisen*

passivity [pæ'siviti] *Teilnahmslosigkeit*

momentary ['mouməntəri] *vorübergehend*

disturb [dis'təːb] *stören*

magic ['mædʒik] *Zauberei*

Paule stopped his pacing in mid career and looked at the wall. He seemed to be speaking to himself.

"Jauntley was murdered at 8.30 exactly. No outside power could have reached him in the Bank vault. So that power must have been already with him, whatever it was. It wasn't a capsule or a pilule–and it was a power that knew Greenwich Mean Time."

With a sudden dart Paule strode across the room to the little table at the foot of the slab on which Jauntley's clothes and effects were ranged. His long white fingers dabbled among them for a moment, then he lifted up the dead man's wrist-watch, a glittering toy on a chromium-plated strap.

"Logically he should have been killed by this!"

"But how, Paule?"

Paule did not answer. He took a penknife and attempted to open the back of the watch. "Queer," he muttered, and pulled out a magnifying glass. "What do you make of that? The lid's brazed on!"

Then he gave a low whistle. "Look!"

Hamerton went to his side and peered through the glass, following Paule's pointing finger. "Why, it's only a pit in the chromium plating at the back. Your often get those flaws."

"Doesn't look like a pit to me. However, let's set the watch to 8.29, and see what happens.

They waited.

in mid career [kə'riə] *mitten im Laufen*

dart [dɑːt] *Satz, Sprung*
strode [stroud] *schritt*

dabble ['dæbl] *hier: wühlen*
lift up [lift] *hochheben*
wrist-watch ['ristwɔtʃ] *Armbanduhr*
glitter ['glitə] *glitzern*
toy [tɔi] *Spielzeug*
chromium-plated ['kroumjəm'pleitid] *verchromt*
strap [stræp] *Riemen, Band*
logically ['lɔdʒikəli] *logischerweise*
penknife ['pennaif] *Taschenmesser*
attempt [ə'tempt] *versuchen*
queer [kwiə] *merkwürdig*
magnifying glass ['mægnifaiiŋ] *Vergrößerungsglas*
lid [lid] *Deckel*
braze [breiz] *löten*
low [lou] *leise*
whistle ['wisl] *Pfiff*
peer [piə] *spähen, gucken*
pit [pit] *Vertiefung*
flaw [flɔː] *Fehler*
set *hier: stellen*

Paule gave a gasp. "See that!"

From the pit a tiny sliver of wire, hardly visible even under the glass, had darted out and vanished again.

"A sting!" breathed Paule. "A poisoned sting! And coated with Martellin, or I'm no policeman. Can you find if it is, Sir Charles?"

"I think so," said the pathologist, holding the watch gingerly by the strap. "I suppose there's a little reservoir of it inside through which the needle affair passes. The simplest way would be to try it on a live animal, but I don't like using them if I can help it. However, I think I can produce something from my bag of tricks that will serve the purpose. Yes, here's a section of living heart muscle in solution." His expert fingers ranged the object deftly before the policemen. "I set the watch to the critical time again, and as the sting comes out, there, I dab it with this wet camel-hair brush. So! As a result, the brush is loaded with whatever poison is on the sting, provided it's water-soluble, and Martellin is. Now I dip the brush in this solution, and stir. Ah!"

Before their astonished eyes the pale section of muscle had contracted convulsively.

Paule's hand quivered with excitement as he picked up the fatal watch.

"How diabolically ingenious. I suppose it has been substituted for his ordinary watch, and is an exact imitation of it. Where was Jauntley's watch put at night?"

gasp [gɑːsp] *schweres Atmen*
tiny ['taini] *winzig*
sliver ['slivə] *Splitter, Span*
visible ['vizibl] *sichtbar*
dart [dɑːt] *schießen, schnellen*
vanish ['væniʃ] *verschwinden*
sting [stiŋ] *Stachel*
breathe [briːð] *hauchen*
coat [kout] *bedecken, überziehen*
gingerly ['dʒindʒəli] *behutsam*
reservoir ['rezəvwɑː] *Behälter*
needle ['niːdl] *Nadel*
live [laiv] *lebendig*
animal ['æniməl] *Tier*
if I can help it *wenn ich es vermeiden kann*
produce [prə'djuːs] *hervorholen*
serve [səːv] *dienen*
purpose ['pəːpəs] *Zweck*
section ['sekʃən] *Abschnitt, Teil*
muscle ['mʌsl] *Muskel*
solution [sə'luːʃən] *Lösung*
expert ['ekspəːt] *geschickt*
deft [deft] *gewandt*
critical ['kritikəl] *kritisch*
dab [dæb] *betupfen*
wet [wet] *feucht*
camel ['kæməl] *Kamel*
brush [brʌʃ] *Pinsel*
as a result [ri'zʌlt] *die Folge ist, daß*
loaded ['loudid] *hier: benetzt*
provided [prə'vaidid] *vorausgesetzt (daß)*
soluble ['sɔljubl] *löslich*
dip [dip] *(ein)tauchen*

astonish [əs'tɔniʃ] *erstaunen*
contract [kən'trækt] *sich zusammenziehen*
convulsive [kən'vʌlsiv] *krampfartig*
quiver ['kwivə] *zittern*
excitement [ik'saitmənt] *Erregung*

Briggs was recalled and remembered that the watch had been kept on a little table, with the dead man's money, in the dressing-room, beneath a window.

"An open window, Briggs?"

Briggs nodded.

Hamerton sighed. "Knowledge of the dead man's habits there. The watch was changed for another through the open window I expect, with a hooked stick or lazy tongs, while the police were guarding him in the other room! All right, Briggs, you couldn't have foreseen it."

"I can't help feeling," said Paule thoughtfully, "that X. K. has not quite finished with us. This is obviously meant to be the neatest job he has ever done, but he has left one rough edge, this watch. I admit he never guessed we should find out that Jauntley did not die of heart failure, but the fact remains we have this watch, and some day, perhaps, with the watch wound up, and the hands at 8.30, the sting might be noticed..."

"What are you getting at, Paule?" said Hamerton, puzzled.

"I have a kind of hunch that X. K. will try to get this watch back!"

"If he does!" exclaimed Hamerton grimly.

"We must give him some incentive, though," said Paule. "What about getting this story in the evening papers: that it has been discovered that Sir Richard Jauntley has been poisoned by Martellin, and the police are now hoping to dis-

diabolical [daiə'bɔlikəl] *teuflisch*
ingenious [in'dʒiːnjəs] *genial, sinnreich*
imitation [imi'teiʃən] *Nachahmung*

remember [ri'membə] *sich erinnern*
kept [kept] *aufbewahrt*

dressing-room ['dresiŋ-rum] *Ankleidezimmer*
beneath [bi'niːθ] *unter(halb)*

nod [nɔd] *nicken*
sigh [sai] *seufzen*
knowledge ['nɔlidʒ] *Kenntnis*
habit ['hæbit] *Gewohnheit*
change for [tʃeindʒ] *austauschen gegen*
expect F [iks'pekt] *vermuten*
hooked [hukt] *hakenförmig, mit einem Haken*
lazy tongs *Pl.* ['leizi 'tɔŋz] *ausdehnbare Gelenkzange*
foreseen [fɔː'siːn] *vorausgesehen*
obvious ['ɔbviəs] *offensichtlich*
this is meant to be [ment] *dies soll ... sein*
neat [niːt] *sauber, geschickt*
rough edge ['rʌf 'edʒ] *„Haken"*
failure ['feiljə] *Schwäche*
wound up [waund] *aufgezogen*
notice ['noutis] *bemerken, beachten*
get at *hier: anspielen auf*
puzzled ['pʌzld] *verwirrt*
a kind of hunch F [hʌntʃ] *so eine Ahnung*
incentive [in'sentiv] *Anreiz*
though F. *allerdings*

cover how the poison was administered?"

The evening papers splashed this discovery, accompanied by guarded interviews with medical correspondents, most of them a little out of their depth with a new drug.

And then the phone rang in Hamerton's office.

"Superintendent Hamerton? Lady Jauntley speaking. I have just remembered two or three trinkets of sentimental value that poor Richard had with him when he died. A locket with my portrait in, for instance, pinned inside his waistcoat pocket. I wonder if I could send someone down for them?"

Hamerton agreed, replaced the phone, and stared incredulously at Paule.

"Lady Jauntley! Trying to get the watch back!"

Then he added: "But that would explain everything! The inside knowledge. The O.H.M.S. letters!"

Paule smiled. "Have you met Lady Jauntley?"

"Yes."

"I ask you, Hamerton, could she possibly be X. K.? I've got a strange feeling, through brooding over this case, that I know exactly the kind of man X. K. is. I feel I shall recognize him at once. I may be wrong; but I'd be ready to stake my reputation it's not Lady Jauntley, nor any kind of woman I've met, for that matter!"

"Well, what shall we do about Lady Jauntley's request?"

"Wait and see!"

splash [splæʃ] *hier: verbreiten*
discovery [dis'kʌvəri] *Entdeckung*
interview ['intəvjuː] *Interview*
correspondent [kɔris'pɔndənt] *Berichterstatter*
out of one's depth [depθ] *ratlos, unsicher*
phone F [foun] = telephone
rang [ræŋ] *läutete*
superintendent *BE* [sjuːprin'tendənt] *Polizeichef*
trinket ['triŋkit] *(wertloses) Schmuckstück*
sentimental value [senti'mentl 'vælju] *Liebhaberwert*
locket ['lɔkit] *Medaillon*
portrait ['pɔːtrit] *Porträt*
pin [pin] *anstecken*
waistcoat ['weiskout] *Weste*
I wonder if I could ['wʌndə] *könnte ich vielleicht ...?*
agree [ə'griː] *zustimmen*
replace the phone [ri'pleis] *(Hörer) auflegen*
incredulous [in'kredjuləs] *ungläubig*
inside ['in'said] *hier: genau, intim*
met [met] *begegnet*
possibly ['pɔsibli] *möglicherweise*
strange [streindʒ] *merkwürdig*
brood [bruːd] *brüten, grübeln*
what kind of [kaind] *was für ein*
recognize ['rekəgnaiz] *erkennen*
stake [steik] *aufs Spiel setzen*
reputation [repjuː'teiʃən] *(guter) Ruf*
for that matter *was das anbetrifft*
request [ri'kwest] *Bitte, Ersuchen*
wait and see *abwarten*

The table with Sir Richard Jauntley's belongings on it had been moved into Hamerton's office. Half an hour later there was a discreet tap, and Higgins, Jauntley's servant, was shown in. He was dressed in black, with a pale thin face, and a high bald forehead backed by a few strings of dark hair.

Paule stepped forward.

"What precisely are the things you want, Higgins?"

"These, sir!" Higgins held out a slip of paper. On it was written in Lady Jauntley's handwriting:

"Little gold locket.
Silver propelling pencil.
Signet-ring.
Wrist-watch."

Paule looked up suddenly from the slip of paper and caught the eyes of the man-servant. They were black with dilated pupils, in which Paule could see his own inverted image. In that moment he had the odd sensation of being in the presence of someone being different in kind from himself. More intelligent perhaps, more powerful, and yet pitifully lacking in some obvious quality every child possesses.

"Morality, I suppose," thought Paule afterwards.

In that moment Paule knew he was in the presence of X. K.

Then Higgins's eyes dropped.

"Please wait in the next room, Higgins. Take him in, Briggs!" said Paule, giving the constable the secret signal which indicated that the wit-

belongings *Pl.* [bi'lɔŋiŋz] *Habseligkeiten*
move [muːv] *fortschaffen*
discreet [dis'kriːt] *vorsichtig*
tap [tæp] *Klopfen*
servant ['səːvənt] *Diener*
show in *hereinführen*
bald [bɔːld] *kahl*
forehead ['fɔrid] *Stirn*
back [bæk] *(nach hinten) begrenzen, einrahmen*
string [striŋ] *hier: Strähne*
held out [held] *hinhalten*
slip [slip] *Zettel*

locket ['lɔkit] *Medaillon*
propelling pencil [prə'peliŋ 'pensl] *Drehbleistift*
signet-ring ['signitriŋ] *Siegelring*

dilate [dai'leit] *erweitern*
pupil ['pjuːpl] *Pupille*
invert [in'vəːt] *umkehren*
sensation [sen'seiʃən] *Gefühl*
presence ['prezns] *Nähe*
being ['biːiŋ] *Geschöpf*
different in kind from *von anderer Art als*
pitiful ['pitiful] *bemitleidenswert*
he is lacking in ['lækiŋ] *ihm fehlt es an*
quality ['kwɔliti] *Eigenschaft*
morality [mə'ræliti] *Moral*

drop [drɔp] *sich senken*

indicate ['indikeit] *anzeigen*
witness ['witnis] *Zeuge*

ness was not to be allowed to leave without permission.

"We have to get an authorization," he explained to Higgins.

"What on earth did you do that for?" asked Hamerton, a little reprovingly, for Paule was technically his junior, though the difference in authority was so slight as to receive no more than the tribute of an intermittent deference from Paule.

"That man is X. K.!" said Paule.

"But how do you know?"

"As one knows things like that. In my bones!"

"But can you prove it?" asked Hamerton reasonably.

"That's a different matter," said Paule, running his hands through his red hair. "May I ring up Lady Jauntley?"

He asked the astonished widow a number of questions. How did the idea of sending for the locket come to her? Well, as a matter of fact, in conversation with Higgins. Did he suggest it? Good gracious, no, it was her suggestion, she was sure. Did Higgins suggest the items to be retrieved? He had helped her. The wrist-watch? She could not remember.

Paule banged down the receiver a little angrily.

"What a psychologist the man is! Of course the suggestion came from him. But he naturally led Lady Jauntley on in conversation so that it seemed to come from her. Her evidence would count for nothing in the

permission [pə'miʃən] *Erlaubnis*
authorization [ɔːθərai'zeiʃən] *Genehmigung, Ermächtigung*
what on earth? F *was in aller Welt?*
reprove [ri'pruːv] *mißbilligen*
technically ['teknikəli] *eigentlich*
his junior ['dʒuːnjə] *ihm untergeordnet*
authority [ɔː'θɔriti] *Autorität, Amtsgewalt*
slight [slait] *gering*
as to *(so) daß*
receive [ri'siːv] *erhalten*
tribute ['tribjuːt] *Anerkennung*
intermittent [intəː'mitənt] *zeitweilig*
deference ['defərəns] *Ehrerbietung*

(I feel it) in my bones *Pl.* [bounz] *(ich habe) so e-e Ahnung*
prove [pruːv] *beweisen*
reasonably ['riːznəbli] *vernünftigerweise*
run one's hand through one's hair *sich mit der Hand durch die Haare fahren*
ring up [riŋ] *anrufen*

widow ['widou] *Witwe*
as a matter of fact *eigentlich*
conversation [kɔnvə'seiʃən] *Gespräch*
suggest [sə'dʒest] *anregen*
good gracious! ['greiʃəs] *du lieber Himmel!*
suggestion [sə'dʒestʃən] *Vorschlag*
item ['aitəm] *einzelner Gegenstand*
retrieve [ri'triːv] *zurückholen*
bang down [bæŋ] *hinknallen*
receiver [ri'siːvə] *(Telefon)Hörer*
psychologist [sai'kɔlədʒist] *Psychologe*

witness-box. In fact she'd be evidence for the defence."

"How can we get him, Hamerton?" he finished desperately.

"Hold him for three or four hours! Meanwhile I'll get every man I can spare on the job."

Higgins was, in fact, held for forty-eight hours. During that time his rooms, his clothes, and his past were searched expertly and exhaustively. And nothing came of it. His clothes and rooms contained nothing to connect him with X. K. He was the son of poor but honest parents, and had been in service all his life.

"But, of course," said Paule, "that is just what you'd expect of X. K. He's a genius, a criminal artist, with more cunning and less morals than any man. He probably delighted in seeming an ordinary humdrum servant, attentive and respectful, and meanwhile, in his hours off, exercising his fiendish power over the persons and properties of the greatest in the land. In his time off he's someone we can't even guess, with a huge fortune, and perhaps the most respected name. How can we trace the connection without a clue? Higgins can become X. K. in such a way as not to leave his tracks behind!"

"Well, what are we to do, my lad?" asked Hamerton.

"Let him go, I suppose," answered Paule bitterly. "Let him go on murdering and terrorizing, while we stand helpless. Do you realize what X. K.'s release means, Hamerton? The end of law and order! The rule of

evidence ['evidəns] *Zeugenaussage*
count for nothing *nichts wert sein*

witness-box *BE* ['witnisbɔks] *Zeugenstand*
defence [di'fens] *Verteidigung*
desperate ['despərit] *verzweifelt*
meanwhile ['mi:n'wail] *inzwischen*
spare [spɛə] *entbehren*
past [pa:st] *Vergangenheit*
expert ['ekspə:t] *fachkundig*
exhaustive [ig'zɔ:stiv] *erschöpfend*
contain [kən'tein] *enthalten*
connect [kə'nekt] *in Verbindung bringen*
honest ['ɔnist] *rechtschaffen*
service ['sə:vis] *Dienst*
expect [iks'pekt] *erwarten*
genius ['dʒi:njəs] *Genie*
criminal ['kriminl] *verbrecherisch*
cunning ['kʌniŋ] *List, Verschlagenheit*
morals *Pl.* ['mɔrəlz] *Moral*
delight in [di'lait] *Freude haben an*
humdrum ['hʌmdrʌm] *alltäglich*
attentive [ə'tentiv] *aufmerksam*
hours off *freie Stunden, freie Zeit*
exercise ['eksəsaiz] *anwenden*
fiendish ['fi:ndiʃ] *teuflisch*
property ['prɔpəti] *Vermögen*
fortune ['fɔ:tʃən] *Vermögen*
trace [treis] *aufspüren*
clue [klu:] *Schlüssel, Fingerzeig*
track [træk] *Spur*
lad [læd] *Junge, Bursche*

the criminal! For thousands of imitators will rise up, inspired by X. K.'s success. And thousands of rich men will fear them, terrified by Jauntley's death!" There was a silence. Paule's chair clattered suddenly. "I've an idea! Have him sent in!"

Higgins came in, quiet, obsequious, eyes deferentially downcast. "I hope my innocence is proved, sir. The suggestion was a terrible shock, and me so devoted to my master!"

"And so clever at reading his confidential reports and using his postbag!" exploded Hamerton.

Higgins looked at the policeman with a humble smile.

"Really, sir, as if I should dream of such a thing!"

Paule ignored Hamerton's outburst. He was swinging a glittering wristwatch gently by its strap. "Higgins, would you have any objection to putting on this watch?"

Higgins looked at the watch and then into Paule's eyes. Both men were silent for a full minute. It seemed to Hamerton as if he were a spectator at a duel between Paule and Higgins, fought with invisible weapons of the mind, and that he was no more than a piece of furniture, playing not even the part of a property in the drama enacted before his eyes.

"No; why should I object?" Higgins said at last.

"I thought you would have no objection. No innocent man could. Hold out your wrist."

terrorize ['terəraiz] *einschüchtern*
realize ['riəlaiz] *sich klarmachen*
release [ri'liːs] *Freilassung*

---

inspire [in'spaiə] *anregen*
success [sək'ses] *Erfolg*
terrify ['terifai] *verängstigen*
silence ['sailəns] *Schweigen*
clatter ['klætə] *klappern*
have him sent in *laß ihn hereinkommen*
quiet ['kwaiət] *ruhig*
obsequious [əb'siːkwiəs] *unterwürfig*
deferential [defə'renʃəl] *ehrerbietig*
downcast ['daunkaːst] *niedergeschlagen*
innocence ['inəsns] *Schuldlosigkeit*
suggestion [sə'dʒestʃən] *Vermutung, Verdacht*
devoted [di'voutid] *ergeben*
confidential [kɔnfi'denʃəl] *vertraulich*
report [ri'pɔːt] *Bericht*
explode [iks'ploud] *herausplatzen*
humble ['hʌmbl] *bescheiden*
ignore [ig'nɔː] *nicht beachten*
outburst ['autbəːst] *(Wut)Ausbruch*
gentle ['dʒentl] *leicht, ruhig*
objection [əb'dʒekʃən] *Einwand*
be silent ['sailənt] *schweigen*
spectator [spek'teitə] *Zuschauer*
piece of furniture ['fəːnitʃə] *Möbelstück*
part [paːt] *Rolle*
property ['prɔpəti] *Requisit*
drama ['draːmə] *Schauspiel*
enact [i'nækt] *aufführen*
object [əb'dʒekt] *etw. dagegen haben*

"Silly, it seems to me," said Higgins, his eyes as unblinking as a lizard's.

"Hold out your wrist!"

Higgins extended it.

"It's a dreadful thing to fall under suspicion, Higgins," went on Paule dreamily. "Particularly suspicion of being X. K. Think of being shadowed everywhere, day and night. Never a moment's peace. Everything pried into. No more liberty to lord it over the lords of the earth. Never a minute's respite to slip into your other personality. Always feeling an inferior, hunted creature."

"I don't know what you are talking about," said Higgins coldly. He looked down at the watch. "Look 'ere, this thing's wrong. It says twenty-eight minutes past eight; and it's only quarter past four by your clock!"

Suddenly Hamerton perceived the full implications of this puzzling conversation. Paule had trapped Higgins. If Higgins was innocent, he would be unconcerned at the progress of the hands to the fatal hour. If he were guilty, however, he would be bound, on pain of death, to snatch it off before the time of striking. What a risk! Supposing Higgins were innocent. But of course Paule would have put the sting out of action. The test was a brilliant bluff.

"Never mind about the hands," Paule was saying sharply. "The watch is going—that's the great thing. X. K. was a great man," Paule went on in the dreamy tone again, "and I

wrist [rist] *Handgelenk*
silly ['sili] *dumm, albern*
unblinking [ʌn'bliŋkiŋ] *starr, ohne Blinzeln*
lizard ['lizəd] *Eidechse*
extend [iks'tend] *ausstrecken*
suspicion [səs'piʃən] *Verdacht*
particularly [pə'tikjuləli] *besonders*
shadow ['ʃædou] *beschatten, verfolgen*
pry into [prai] *nachschnüffeln*
lord it over [lɔːd] *sich j-m gegenüber als Herr aufspielen*
respite ['respait] *Frist*
slip [slip] *schlüpfen*
inferior [in'fiəriə] *minderwertig*
'ere = here
say *hier: zeigen auf*
by *nach*
perceive [pə'siːv] *begreifen*
implication [impli'keiʃən] *Folge(rung)*
puzzling ['pʌzliŋ] *rätselhaft*
trap [træp] *fangen, hereinlegen*
unconcerned ['ʌnkən'səːnd] *unberührt, unbesorgt*
progress ['prougres] *vorrücken*
hand [hænd] *Zeiger*
guilty ['gilti] *schuldig*
be bound to do s. th. [baund] *zwangsläufig etwas tun müssen*
on pain of death [deθ] *bei Todesstrafe*
snatch off [snætʃ] *abreißen*
strike [straik] *treffen, stechen*
risk [risk] *Wagnis*
out of action ['ækʃən] *außer Betrieb*
test [test] *Probe*
never mind [maind] *kümmern Sie sich nicht um*

don't think that kind of life would appeal to him—to be a harried, hunted creature, after frightening the greatest people in the world. He was an artist, was X. K., and knew when a work of art was complete."

A wild gleam kindled in Higgins eyes. His lips became chips of stone. The thin pale face changed unbelievably, became the face of a maniac, of a saint who by some incredible combination of circumstances has irretrievably damned himself.

"Yes, he was an artist," he shouted, "the greatest criminal the world has ever known!"

His face flushed, and changed again; his arms sawed at the air; he slid off his chair. After a twitch or two he was motionless—dead.

Hamerton gazed at the body in horror. "Paule, what have you done? I thought it was a trap! That he'd prove himself guilty by taking off the watch!"

"Nothing of the sort," said Paule. The tension of his contest had left him lax and depressed. "I knew Higgins was X. K. and he knew that I knew. I was trying to persuade him that though we couldn't prove him guilty, it was better that he should die than be subjected for the rest of his life to our attentions. You see, I was banking on the colossal vanity of the criminal. It was a bluff, for we couldn't have fulfilled our threat. But I won."

"We'd better write our report," added Paule. "While being cross-examined, the prisoner made a con-

appeal [ə'piːl] *gefallen, reizen*
harry ['hæri] *quälen*
frighten ['fraitn] *in Schrecken versetzen*
art [ɑːt] *Kunst*
complete [kəm'pliːt] *vollkommen, -endet*
gleam [gliːm] *Schimmer*
kindle [kindl] *aufflammen*
chip [tʃip] *Splitter*
unbelievable [ʌnbi'liːvəbl] *unglaublich*
maniac ['meiniæk] *Wahnsinniger*
saint [seint] *Heilige(r)*
incredible [in'kredəbl] *unvorstellbar*
irretrievable [iri'triːvəbl] *unrettbar*
damn [dæm] *verdammen*
flush [flʌʃ] *erröten*
saw at the air [sɔː] *(mit den Händen) herumfuchteln*
slid [slid] *glitt*
twitch [twitʃ] *Zuckung*
motionless ['mouʃənlis] *reglos*
gaze [geiz] *starren*
horror ['hɔrə] *Entsetzen*
tension ['tenʃən] *Spannung*
contest ['kɔntest] *Kampf*
lax [læks] *schlaff*
depressed [di'prest] *niedergeschlagen*
persuade [pə'sweid] *überzeugen*
subject [səb'dʒekt] *unterwerfen*
attention [ə'tenʃən] *Aufmerksamkeit*
bank on [bæŋk] *bauen auf*
colossal F [kə'lɔsl] *kolossal, enorm*
vanity ['væniti] *Eitelkeit*
fulfil [ful'fil] *erfüllen, ausführen*
won [wʌn] *gewann*
cross-examine ['krɔs ig'zæmin] *ins Kreuzverhör nehmen*
prisoner ['priznə] *Angeklagte(r)*

fession and killed himself with a watch snatched from the table, which thus proved to be the instrument of Sir Richard Jauntley's death. – The report will be quite true, because Higgins's last words were a confession."

No one besides Hamerton ever knew of what the Superintendent called "Paule's Private Murder".

"But I tell you it was suicide," Paul would reply, not too well pleased with this joke.

X. K. was never heard of again, but a certain hotel mourned the absence of a mysterious stranger, who used to appear suddenly, spend lavishly, and disappear again.

confession [kən'feʃən] *Geständnis*
besides [bi'saidz] *außer*
suicide ['sjuisaid] *Selbstmord*
be pleased with [pli:zd] *Gefallen finden an*
joke [dʒouk] *Spaß, Scherz*
mourn [mɔ:n] *beklagen*
absence ['æbsəns] *Fernbleiben*
mysterious [mis'tiəriəs] *geheimnisvoll*
stranger ['streindʒə] *Fremder*
appear [ə'piə] *erscheinen*
spend [spend] *Geld ausgeben*
lavish ['læviʃ] *verschwenderisch*
disappear [disə'piə] *verschwinden*

(From: Windsor Magazine. London, March, Ward, Lock & Co.)